History of the Fabian Society

The Origins of English Socialism

Edward R Pease
(Secretary for 25 Years)

Red and Black Publishers, St Petersburg, Florida

First published in New York in 1916

Library of Congress Cataloging-in-Publication Data

Pease, Edward R. (Edward Reynolds), 1857-
  History of the Fabian Society : the origins of English socialism /
Edward R. Pease.
      p. cm.
    "First published in New York in 1916"--T.p. verso.
    ISBN 978-1-934941-32-4
  1. Fabian Society (Great Britain) 2. Socialism--Great Britain. I.
Title.
    HX11.F5P43 2008
    335'.14--dc22

                                                    2008021851

Red and Black Publishers, PO Box 7542, St Petersburg, Florida, 33734
Contact us at: info@RedandBlackPublishers.com

Printed and manufactured in the United States of America

Contents

Chapter I   The Sources of Fabian Socialism

The ideas of the early eighties – The epoch of Evolution – Sources of Fabian ideas – Positivism – Henry George – John Stuart Mill – Robert Owen – Karl Marx – The Democratic Federation – "The Christian Socialist" – Thomas Davidson.

"Britain as a whole never was more tranquil and happy," said the *Spectator*, then the organ of sedate Liberalism and enlightened Progress, in the summer of 1882. "No class is at war with society or the government: there is no disaffection anywhere, the Treasury is fairly full, the accumulations of capital are vast"; and then the writer goes on to compare Great Britain with Ireland, at that time under the iron heel of coercion, with Parnell and hundreds of his followers in jail, whilst outrages and murders, like those of Maamtrasma, were almost everyday occurrences.

Some of the problems of the early (eighteen)-eighties are with us yet. Ireland is still a bone of contention between political parties: the Channel tunnel is no nearer completion: and then as now, when other topics are exhausted, the *Spectator* can fill up its columns with Thought Transference and Psychical Research.

But other problems which then were vital, are now almost forgotten. Electric lighting was a doubtful novelty: Mr. Bradlaugh's refusal to take the oath excited a controversy which now seems incredible. Robert Louis Stevenson can no longer be adequately described as an "accomplished writer," and the introduction of female clerks into the postal service by Mr. Fawcett has ceased to raise alarm lest the courteous practice of always allowing ladies to be victors in an argument should perforce be abandoned.

But in September of the same year we find a cloud on the horizon, the prelude of a coming storm. The Trade Union Congress had just been held and the leaders of the working classes, with apparently but little discussion, had passed a resolution asking the Government to institute an enquiry with a view to relaxing the stringency of Poor Law administration. This, said the *Spectator*, is beginning "to tamper with natural conditions." "There is no logical halting-place between the theory that it is the duty of the State to make the poor comfortable, and socialism."

Another factor in the thought of those days attracted but little attention in the Press, though there is a long article in the *Spectator* at the beginning of 1882 on "the ever-increasing wonder" of that strange faith, "Positivism." It is difficult for the present generation to realise how large a space in the minds of the young men of the eighties was occupied by the religion invented by Auguste Comte. Of this however more must be said on a later page.

But perhaps the most significant feature in the periodical literature of the time is what it omits. April, 1882, is memorable for the death of Charles Darwin, incomparably the greatest of nineteenth-century Englishmen, if greatness be measured by the effects of his work on the thought of the world. The *Spectator* printed a secondary article which showed some appreciation of the event. But in the monthly reviews it passed practically unnoticed. It is true that Darwin was buried in Westminster Abbey, but even in 1882, twenty-three years after the publication of the *Origin of Species*, evolution was regarded as a somewhat dubious theorem which respectable people were wise to ignore.

In the monthly reviews we find the same odd mixture of articles apposite to present problems, and articles utterly out of date. The organisation of agriculture is a perennial, and Lady Verney's "Peasant Proprietorship in France" (*Contemporary*, January, 1882), Mr. John Rae's "Co-operative Agriculture in Germany" (*Contemporary*, March, 1882), and Professor Sedley Taylor's "Profit-Sharing in Agriculture" (*Nineteenth Century*, October, 1882) show that change in the methods of exploiting the soil is leaden-footed and lagging.

Problems of another class, centring round "the Family," present much the same aspect now as they did thirty years ago. In his "Infant Mortality and Married Women in Factories," Professor Stanley Jevons (*Contemporary*, January, 1882) proposes that mothers of children under three years of age should be excluded from factories, and we are at present perhaps even farther from general agreement whether any measure on these lines ought to be adopted.

But when we read the articles on Socialism — more numerous than might be expected at that early date — we are in another world. Mr. Samuel Smith, M.P., writing on "Social Reform" in the *Nineteenth Century* for May, 1883, says that: "Our country is still comparatively free from Communism and Nihilism and similar destructive movements, but who can tell how long this will continue? We have a festering mass of human wretchedness in all our great towns, which is the natural hotbed of such anarchical movements: all the great continental countries are full of this explosive material. Can we depend on our country keeping free from the infection when we have far more poverty in our midst than the neighbouring European States?" Emigration and temperance reform, he thinks, may avert the danger.

The Rev. Samuel (later Canon) Barnett in the same review a month earlier advocated Free Libraries and graduated taxation to pay for free education, under the title of "Practicable Socialism." In April, 1883, Emile de Lavelaye described with alarm the "Progress of Socialism." "On the Continent," he wrote, "Socialism is said to be everywhere." To it he attributed with remarkable inaccuracy, the agrarian movement in Ireland, and with it he connected the fact that Henry George's new book, *Progress and Poverty*, was selling by thousands "in an ultra popular form" in the back streets and alleys of England. And then he goes on to allude to Prince Bismarck's "abominable proposition to create a fund for pensioning invalid workmen by a monopoly of tobacco"!

Thirty years ago politics were only intermittently concerned with social problems. On the whole the view prevailed, at any rate amongst the leaders, that Government should interfere in such matters as little as possible. Pauperism was still to be stamped out by ruthless deterrence: education had been only recently and reluctantly taken in hand: factory inspection alone was an accepted State function. Lord Beaconsfield was dead and he had forgotten his zeal for social justice long before he attained power. Gladstone, then in the zenith of his fame, never took any real interest in social questions as we now understand them. Lord Salisbury was an aristocrat and thought as an aristocrat. John Bright viewed industrial life from the standpoint of a Lancashire mill-owner. William Edward Forster, the creator of national education, a Chartist in his youth, had become the gaoler of Parnell and the protagonist of coercion in Ireland. Joseph Chamberlain alone seemed to realise the significance of the social problem, and unhappily political events were soon to deflect his career from what then seemed to be its appointed course.

The political parties therefore offered very little attraction to the young men of the early eighties, who, viewing our social system with the fresh eyes of youth, saw its cruelties and its absurdities and judged them, not as older men, by comparison with the worse cruelties and greater absurdities of earlier days, but by the standard of common fairness and common sense, as set out in the lessons they had learned in their schools, their universities, and their churches.

It is nowadays not easy to recollect how wide was the intellectual gulf which separated the young generation of that period from their parents. *The Origin of Species*, published in 1859, inaugurated an intellectual revolution such as the world had not known since Luther nailed his Theses to the door of All Saints' Church at Wittenberg. The older folk as a rule refused to accept or to consider the new doctrine. I recollect a botanical Fellow of the Royal Society who, in 1875, told me that he had no opinions on Darwin's hypothesis. The young men of the time I am describing grew up with the new ideas and accepted them as a matter of course. Herbert Spencer, then deemed the greatest of English thinkers, was pointing out in portentous phraseology the enormous significance of Evolution. Professor Huxley, in brilliant essays, was turning to ridicule the simple-minded credulity of Gladstone and his contemporaries. Our parents, who read neither Spencer nor Huxley, lived in an intellectual world which bore no relation to our own; and cut adrift as we were from the intellectual moorings of our upbringings, recognising, as we did, that the older men were useless as guides in religion, in science, in philosophy because they knew not evolution, we also felt instinctively that we could accept nothing on trust from those who still believed that the early chapters of Genesis accurately described the origin of the universe, and that we had to discover somewhere for ourselves what were the true principles of the then recently invented science of sociology.

One man there was who professed to offer us an answer, Auguste Comte. He too was pre-Darwinian, but his philosophy accepted science, future as well as past. John Stuart Mill, whose word on his own subjects was then almost law, wrote of him with respectful admiration. His followers were known to number amongst them some of the ablest thinkers of the day. The "Religion of Humanity" offered solutions for all the problems that faced us. It suggested a new heaven, of a sort, and it proposed a new earth, free from all the inequalities of wealth, the preventable suffering, the reckless waste of effort, which we saw around us. At any rate, it was worth examination; and most of the free-thinking men of that period read the "Positive Polity" and the other writings of the founder, and spent some Sunday mornings at the little conventicle in Lamb's Conduit Street, or attended on Sunday evenings the Newton Hall lectures of Frederic Harrison.

Few could long endure the absurdities of a made-up theology and a make-believe religion: and the Utopia designed by Comte was as impracticable and unattractive as Utopias generally are. But the critical and destructive part of the case was sound enough. Here was a man who challenged the existing order of society and pronounced it wrong. It was in his view based on conventions, on superstitions, on regulations which were all out of date; society should be reorganised in the light of pure reason; the anarchy of competition must be brought to an end; mankind should recognise that order, good sense, science, and, he added, religion freed from superstition, could turn the world into a place where all might live together in comfort and happiness.

Positivism proposed to attain its Utopia by moralising the capitalists, and herein it showed no advance on Christianity, which for nineteen centuries had in vain preached social obligation to the rich. The new creed could not succeed where the old, with all its tremendous sanctions, had completely failed. We wanted something fresh, some new method of dealing with the inequalities of wealth.

Emile de Lavelaye was quite correct in attributing significance to the publication of *Progress and Poverty*, though the seed sown by Henry George took root, not in the slums and alleys of our cities — no intellectual seed of any sort can germinate in the sickly, sunless atmosphere of slums — but in the minds of people who had sufficient leisure and education to think of other things than breadwinning. Henry George proposed to abolish poverty by political action: that was the new gospel which came from San Francisco in the early eighties. *Progress and Poverty* was published in America in 1879, and its author visited England at the end of 1881. Socialism hardly existed at that time in English-speaking countries, but the early advocates of land taxation were not then, as they usually are now, uncompromising individualists. *Progress and Poverty* gave an extraordinary impetus to the political thought of the time. It proposed to redress the wrongs suffered by the working classes as a whole: the poverty it considered was the poverty of the wage workers as a class, not the destitution of the unfortunate and downtrodden individuals. It did not merely propose, like philanthropy and the Poor Law, to relieve the acute suffering of the outcasts of civilisation, those condemned to wretchedness by the incapacity, the vice, the folly, or the sheer misfortune of themselves or their relations. It suggested a method by which wealth would correspond approximately with worth; by which the reward of labour would go to those that laboured; the idleness alike of rich and poor would cease; the abundant wealth created by modern industry would be distributed with something like fairness and even equality, amongst those who contributed to its production. Above all, this tremendous revolution was to be accomplished by a political method, applicable by a majority of the voters, and capable of being drafted as an Act of Parliament by any competent lawyer.

To George belongs the extraordinary merit of recognising the right way of social salvation. The Socialists of earlier days had proposed segregated communities; the Co-operators had tried voluntary associations; the Positivists advocated moral suasion; the Chartists favoured force, physical or political; the Marxists talked revolution and remembered the Paris Commune. George wrote in a land where the people ruled themselves, not only in fact but also in name. The United States in the seventies was not yet dominated by trusts and controlled by millionaires. Indeed even now that domination and control, dangerous and disastrous as it often is, could not withstand for a moment any widespread uprising of the popular will. Anyway, George recognised that in the Western States political institutions could be moulded to suit the will of the electorate; he believed that the majority desired to seek their own well-being and this could not fail to be also the well-being of the community as a whole. From Henry George I think it may be taken that the early

Fabians learned to associate the new gospel with the old political method.

But when we came to consider the plan proposed by George we quickly saw that it would not carry us far. Land may be the source of all wealth to the mind of a settler in a new country. To those whose working day was passed in Threadneedle Street and Lombard Street, on the floor of the Stock Exchange, and in the Bank of England, land appears to bear no relation at all to wealth, and the allegation that the whole surplus of production goes automatically to the landowners is obviously untrue. George's political economy was old-fashioned or absurd; and his solution of the problem of poverty could not withstand the simplest criticism. Taxation to extinction of the rent of English land would only affect a small fraction of England's wealth.

There was another remedy in the field. Socialism was talked about in the reviews: some of us knew that an obscure Socialist movement was stirring into life in London. And above all John Stuart Mill had spoken very respectfully of Socialism in his *Political Economy*, which then held unchallenged supremacy as an exposition of the science. If, he wrote, "the choice were to be made between Communism [the words Communism and Socialism were interchangeable at that period, e.g. the *Manifesto of the Communist Party*, by Karl Marx and Frederick Engels, 1848] with all its chances, and the present state of society with all its sufferings and injustices, if the institution of private property necessarily carried with it as a consequence that the produce of labour should be apportioned as we now see it almost in inverse proportion to labour, the largest portions to those who have never worked at all, the next largest to those whose work is almost nominal, and so in descending scale, the remuneration dwindling as the work grows harder and more disagreeable until the most fatiguing and exhausting bodily labour cannot count with certainty on being able to earn even the necessities of life; if this or Communism were the alternative, all the difficulties, great or small, of Communism would be but as dust in the balance."

And again in the next paragraph: "We are too ignorant, either of what individual agency in its best form or Socialism in its best form can accomplish, to be qualified to decide which of the two will be the ultimate form of human society."

More than thirty years had passed since this had been written, and whilst the evils of private property, so vividly depicted by Mill, showed no signs of mitigation, the remedies he anticipated had made no substantial progress. The co-operation of the Rochdale Pioneers had proved a magnificent success, but its sphere of operations was now clearly seen to be confined within narrow limits. Profit-sharing then as now was a sickly plant barely kept alive by the laborious efforts of benevolent professors. Mill's indictment of the capitalist system, in regard to its effects on social life, was so powerful, his treatment of the primitive socialism and communism of his day so sympathetic, that it is surprising how little it prepared the way for the reception of the new ideas. But to some of his readers, at any rate, it suggested that there was an alternative to the capitalistic system, and that Socialism or Communism was worthy of examination.

The Socialism of Robert Owen had made a profound impression on the working people of England half a century earlier, but the tradition of it was confined to those who had heard its prophet. Owen, one of the greatest men of his age, had no sense of art; his innumerable writings are unreadable; and both his later excursions into spiritualism, and the failure of his communities and co-operative enterprises, had clouded his reputation amongst those outside the range of his personality. In later years we often came across old men who had sat at his feet, and who rejoiced to hear once more something resembling his teachings: but I do not think that, at the beginning, the Owenite tradition had any influence upon us.

Karl Marx died in London on the 14th March, 1883, but nobody in England was then aware that the greatest figure in international politics had passed away. It is true that Marx had taken a prominent part in founding the International at that historic meeting in St. Martin's Town Hall on September 28th, 1864. The real significance of that episode was over-rated at the time, and when the International disappeared from European politics in 1872 the whole thing was forgotten.

In Germany Marxian Socialism was already a force, and it was attracting attention in England, as we have seen. But the personality of Marx must have been antipathetic to the English workmen whom he knew, or else he failed to make them understand his ideas: at any rate, his socialism fell on deaf ears, and it may be said to have made no lasting impression on the leaders of English working-class thought. Though he was resident in England for thirty-four years, Marx remained a German to the last. His writings were not translated into English at this period, and Mr. Hyndman's *England for All*, published in 1881, which was the first presentation of his ideas in

English, did not even mention his name. This book was in fact an extremely moderate proposal to remedy "something seriously amiss in the conditions of our everyday life," and the immediate programme was no more than an eight hours working day, free and compulsory education, compulsory construction of working-class dwellings, and cheap "transport" for working-class passengers. It was the unauthorised programme of the Democratic Federation which had been founded by Mr. Hyndman in 1881. *Socialism Made Plain*, the social and political Manifesto of the Democratic Federation (undated, but apparently issued in 1883), is a much stronger document. It deals with the distribution of the National Income, giving the workers' share as 300 out of 1300 millions sterling, and demands that the workers should "educate, agitate, organise" in order to get their own. Evidently it attracted some attention, since we find that the second edition of a pamphlet "Reply" by Samuel Smith, M.P., then a person of substantial importance, was issued in January, 1884.

At the end of 1883 Mr. Hyndman published his *Historical Basis of Socialism in England*, which for some time was the text-book of the Democratic Federation, but this, of course, was too late to influence the founders of the Fabian Society.

We were however aware of Marx, and I find that my copy of the French edition of *Das Kapital* is dated 8th October, 1883; but I do not think that any of the original Fabians had read the book or had assimilated its ideas at the time the Society was founded.

To some of those who joined the Society in its early days Christian Socialism opened the way of salvation. *The Christian Socialist* was established by a band of persons some of whom were not Socialist and others not Christian. It claimed to be the spiritual child of the Christian Socialist movement of 1848-52, which again was Socialist only on its critical side, and constructively was merely Co-operative Production by voluntary associations of workmen. Under the guidance of the Rev. Stewart D. Headlam its policy of the revived movement was Land Reform, particularly on the lines of the Single Tax. The introductory article boldly claims the name of Socialist, as used by Maurice and Kingsley: the July number contains a long article by Henry George. In September a formal report is given of the work of the Democratic Federation. In November Christianity and Socialism are said to be convertible terms, and in January, 1884, the clerical view of usury is set forth in an article on the morality of interest. In March Mr. H.H. Champion explains "surplus value," and in April we find a sympathetic review of the *Historic Basis of Socialism*. In April, 1885, appears a long and full report of a lecture by Bernard Shaw to the Liberal and Social Union. The greater part of the paper is filled with Land Nationalisation, Irish affairs—the land agitation in Ireland was then at its height—and the propaganda of Henry George: whilst much space is devoted to the religious aspect of the social problem. Sydney Olivier, before he joined the Fabian Society, was one of the managing group, and amongst others concerned in it were the Rev. C.L. Marson and the Rev. W.E. Moll. At a later period a Christian Socialist Society was formed; but our concern here is with the factors which contributed to the Fabian Society at its start, and it is not necessary to touch on other periods of the movement.

Thomas Davidson was the occasion rather than the cause of the founding of the Fabian Society. His socialism was ethical and individual rather than economic and political. He was spiritually a descendant of the Utopians of Brook Farm and the Phalanstery, and what he yearned for was something in the nature of a community of superior people withdrawn from the world because of its wickedness, and showing by example how a higher life might be led. Probably his Scotch common sense recoiled from definitely taking the plunge: I am not aware that he ever actually proposed that his disciples should form a self-contained community. In a lecture to the New York Fellowship of the New Life, he said, "I shall set out with two assumptions, first, that human life does not consist in material possession; and second, that it does consist in free spiritual activity, of which in this life at least material possession is an essential condition." There is nothing new in this: it is the common basis of all religions and ethical systems. But it needs to be re-stated for each generation, and so stated as to suit each environment. At the time that I am describing Davidson's re-statement appealed to the small circle of his adherents, though the movement which he started had results that he neither expected nor approved.

I have now indicated the currents of thought which contributed to the formation of the Fabian Society, so far as I can recover them from memory and a survey of the periodical literature of the period. I have not included the writings of Ruskin, Socialist in outlook as some of them undoubtedly are, because I think that the value of his social teachings was concealed from most of us at that time by reaction against his religious mediævalism, and indifference to his gospel of art. Books so eminently adapted for young ladies at mid-Victorian schools did not appeal to modernists educated by Comte and Spencer.

Chapter II   The Foundations of the Society: 1883-4

Frank Podmore and Ghost-hunting – Thomas Davidson and his circle – The preliminary meetings – The Fellowship of the New Life – Formation of the Society – The career of the New Fellowship.

In the autumn of 1883 Thomas Davidson paid a short visit to London and held several little meetings of young people, to whom he expounded his ideas of a Vita Nuova, a Fellowship of the New Life. I attended the last of these meetings held in a bare room somewhere in Chelsea, on the invitation of Frank Podmore, whose acquaintance I had made a short time previously. We had become friends through a common interest first in Spiritualism and subsequently in Psychical Research, and it was whilst vainly watching for a ghost in a haunted house at Notting Hill – the house was unoccupied: we had obtained the key from the agent, left the door unlatched, and returned late at night in the foolish hope that we might perceive something abnormal – that he first discussed with me the teachings of Henry George in "Progress and Poverty," and we found a common interest in social as well as psychical progress.

The English organiser or secretary of the still unformed Davidsonian Fellowship was Percival Chubb, then a young clerk in the Local Government Board, and subsequently a lecturer and head of an Ethical Church in New York and St. Louis. Thomas Davidson was about to leave London; and the company he had gathered round him, desirous of further discussing his suggestions, decided to hold another meeting at my rooms. I was at that time a member of the Stock Exchange and lived in lodgings furnished by myself.

Here then on October 24th, 1883, was held the first of the fortnightly meetings, which have been continued with scarcely a break, through nine months of every year, up to the present time. The company that assembled consisted in part of the Davidsonian circle and in part of friends of my own.

The proceedings at this meeting, recorded in the first minute book of the Society in the handwriting of Percival Chubb, were as follows —

"THE NEW LIFE"

"The first general meeting of persons interested in this movement was held at Mr. Pease's rooms, 17 Osnaburgh Street, Regent's Park, on Wednesday the 24th October, 1883. There were present: Miss Ford, Miss Isabella Ford [of Leeds], Mrs. Hinton [widow of James Hinton], Miss Haddon [her sister], Mr., Mrs., and Miss Robins, Maurice Adams, H.H. Champion, Percival A. Chubb, H. Havelock Ellis, J.L. Joynes, Edward R. Pease, Frank Podmore, R.B.P. Frost, and Hamilton Pullen.

"The proceedings were begun by the reading of Mr. Thomas Davidson's paper 'The New Life,' read by him at a former assemblage, and after it of the Draft of a proposed constitution (Sketch No. 2). [This has not been preserved.]

"A general discussion followed on the question as to what was possible of achievement in the way of founding a communistic society whose members should lead the new higher life foreshadowed in the paper just read. The idea of founding a community abroad was generally discredited, and it was generally recognised that it would not be possible to establish here in England any independent community. What could be done perhaps would be for a number of persons in sympathy with the main idea to unite for the purpose of common living as far as possible on a communistic basis, realising amongst themselves the higher life and making it a primary care to provide a worthy education for the young. The members would pursue their present callings in the world, but they would always aim to make the community as far as practicable self-contained and self-supporting, combining perhaps to carry on some common business or businesses.

"It was eventually arranged to further discuss the matter at another meeting which was fixed for a fortnight hence (Wednesday, 7th November). Mr. Podmore consented to ask Miss Owen [afterwards Mrs. Laurence Oliphant] to attend then and narrate the experiences of the New Harmony Community founded by [her grandfather] Robert Owen.

"It was suggested—and the suggestion was approvingly received—that undoubtedly the first thing to be done was for those present to become thoroughly acquainted with each other. A general introduction of each person to the rest of the company was made and the business of the meeting being concluded conversation followed."

On November 7th, the second meeting was held, when a number of new people attended, including Hubert Bland, who, I think, had been one of the original Davidson group. Miss Owen was unable to be present, and a draft constitution was discussed.

"A question was then raised as to the method of conducting the proceedings. The appointment of a chairman was proposed, and Mr. Pease was appointed. It was suggested that resolutions should be passed constituting a society, and, as far as those present were concerned, designating its objects. Some exception was taken to this course as being an undesirable formality not in harmony with the free spirit of the undertaking, but meeting with general approval it was followed.

"After some discussion ... the following resolution was proposed and agreed to—

"That an association be formed whose ultimate aim shall be the reconstruction of Society in accordance with the highest moral possibilities"

A Committee consisting of Messrs. Champion (who was not present), Ellis, Jupp, Podmore, and Chubb, and, failing Champion, Pease was appointed to draw up and submit proposals, and it was resolved for the future to meet on Fridays, a practice which the Society has maintained ever since.

The meeting on November 23rd was attended by thirty-one people, and included Miss Dale Owen, William Clarke, and Frederick Keddell, the first Secretary of the Fabian Society.

H.H. Champion introduced the proposals of the Committee, including the following resolution, which was carried apparently with unanimity —

"The members of the Society assert that the Competitive system assures the happiness and comfort of the few at the expense of the suffering of the many and that Society must be reconstituted in such a manner as to secure the general welfare and happiness."

Then the minutes go on, indicating already a rift in the Society: "As the resolution referred rather to the material or economic aims of the Society and not to its primary spiritual aim, it was agreed that it should stand as No. 3, and that another resolution setting forth the spiritual basis of the Fellowship shall be passed which shall stand as No. 2."

It proved impossible to formulate then and there the spiritual basis of the Society, and after several suggestions had been made a new committee was appointed. Resolution No. 1 had already been deferred.

The next meeting was held on December 7th, when only fifteen were present. Hubert Bland occupied the chair, and Dr. Burns-Gibson introduced a definite plan as follows —

"THE FELLOWSHIP OF NEW LIFE

Object — The cultivation of a perfect character in each and all.

Principle — The subordination of material things to spiritual.

Fellowship — The sole and essential condition of fellowship shall be a single-minded, sincere, and strenuous devotion to the object and principle."

Further articles touched on the formation of a community, the supplanting of the spirit of competition, the highest education of the young, simplicity of living, the importance of manual labour and religious communion. Nine names were attached to this project, including those of Percival Chubb, Havelock Ellis, and William Clarke, and it was announced that a Fellowship would be formed on this basis, whether it was accepted or rejected by the majority. These propositions were discussed and no decision was arrived at.

Up to this point the minutes are recorded in the writing of Percival Chubb. The next entry was made by Frank Podmore, and those after that by Frederick Keddell.

We now arrive at the birthday of the Fabian Society, and the minutes of that meeting must be copied in full—

"Meeting held at 17 Osnaburgh Street, on Friday, 4th January, 1884.

"Present: Mrs. Robins, Miss Robins, Miss Haddon, Miss C. Haddon, Messrs. J. Hunter Watts, Hughes, Bland, Keddell, Pease, Stapleton, Chubb, Burns-Gibson, Swan, Podmore, Estcourt, etc.

"Mr. Bland took the chair at 8.10 p.m.

"After the minutes of the previous meeting had been read and confirmed Dr. Gibson moved the series of resolutions which had been read to the Society at the previous meeting.

"Mr. Podmore moved as an amendment the series of resolutions, copies of which had been circulated amongst the members a few days previously.

"The amendment was carried by 10 votes to 4.

[Presumably the 4 included Burns-Gibson, Chubb, and Estcourt, who signed the defeated resolutions.]

"Mr. Podmore's proposals were then put forward as substantive resolutions and considered seriatim.

"Resolution I—That the Society be called the Fabian Society (as Mr. Podmore explained in allusion to the victorious policy of Fabius Cunctator) was carried by 9 votes to 2.

"Resolution II—That the Society shall not at present pledge its members to any more definite basis of agreement than that contained in the resolution of 23rd November, 1883.

"Carried unanimously.

"Resolution III—In place of Mr. Podmore's first proposal it was eventually decided to modify the resolution of 7th November, 1883, by inserting the words 'to help on' between the words 'shall be' and the words 'the reconstruction.'

"Resolution IV with certain omissions was agreed to unanimously, viz.: That with the view of learning what practical measures to take in this direction the Society should:

"(a.) Hold meetings for discussion, the reading of papers, hearing of reports, etc.

"(b.) Delegate some of its members to attend meetings held on social subjects, debates at Workmen's Clubs, etc., in order that such members may in the first place report to the Society on the proceedings, and in the second place put forward, as occasion serves, the views of the Society.

"(c.) Take measures in other ways, as, for example, by the collection of articles from current literature, to obtain information on all contemporary social movements and social needs.

"Mr. Bland, Mr. Keddell, and Mr. Podmore were provisionally appointed as an Executive Committee, to serve for three months, on the motion of Mr. Pease. A collection was made to provide funds for past expenses: the sum collected amounting to 13s. 9d."

It appears that Mr. Bland on this occasion acted as treasurer, though there is no record of the fact. He was annually re-elected treasurer and a member of the Executive Committee until he retired from both positions in 1911.

Thus the Society was founded. Although it appeared to be the outcome of a division of opinion, this was scarcely in fact the case. All those present became members, and the relations between the Fabian Society and the Fellowship of the New Life were always of a friendly character, though in fact the two bodies had but little in common, and seldom came into contact.

A few words may be devoted to the Fellowship of the New Life, which continued to exist for fifteen years. Its chief achievement was the publication of a quarterly paper called "Seedtime," issued from July, 1889, to February, 1898. The paper contains articles on Ethical Socialism, the Simple Life, Humanitarianism, the Education of Children, and similar subjects. The Society was conducted much on the same lines as the Fabian Society: fortnightly lectures were given in London and reported in "Seedtime."

In 1893 we find in "Seedtime" an Annual Report recording 12 public meetings, 4 social gatherings, a membership of 95, and receipts £73. During this year, 1892-3, J. Ramsay Macdonald, subsequently M.P. and Secretary and Chairman of the Labour Party, was Honorary Secretary, and for some years he was on the Executive. In 1896 the membership was 115 and the income £48.

The most persistent of the organisers of the New Fellowship was J.F. Oakeshott, who was also for many years a member of the Fabian Executive. Corrie Grant, later a well-known Liberal M.P., H.S. Salt of the Humanitarian League, Edward Carpenter, and his brother Captain Carpenter, Herbert Rix, assistant secretary of the Royal Society, Havelock Ellis, and, both before and after her marriage, Mrs. Havelock Ellis (who was Honorary Secretary for some years), are amongst the names which appear in the pages of "Seedtime,"

Mild attempts were made to carry out the Community idea by means of associated colonies (e.g. the members residing near each other) and a co-operative residence at 49 Doughty Street, Bloomsbury; but close association, especially of persons with the strong and independent opinions of the average socialist, promotes discord, and against this the high ideals of the New Fellowship proved no protection. Indeed it is a common experience that the higher the ideal the fiercer the hostilities of the idealists.

At Thornton Heath, near Croydon, the Fellowship conducted for some time a small printing business, and its concern for the right education for the young found expression in a Kindergarten. Later on an Ethical Church and a Boys' Guild were established at Croydon.

Soon afterwards the Fellowship came to the conclusion that its work was done, the last number of "Seedtime" was published, and in 1898 the Society was dissolved.

Chapter III   The Early Days: 1884-6

The use of the word Socialism – Approval of the Democratic Federation – Tract No. 1--The Fabian Motto – Bernard Shaw joins – His first Tract – The Industrial Remuneration Conference – Sidney Webb and Sydney Olivier become members – Mrs. Annie Besant – Shaw's second Tract – The Tory Gold controversy – "What Socialism Is" – The Fabian Conference of 1886--Sidney Webb's first contribution, "The Government Organisation of Unemployed Labour."

The Fabian Society was founded for the purpose of "reconstructing society," based on the competitive system, "in such manner as to secure the general welfare and happiness." It is worth noting that the word "Socialism" had not yet appeared in its records, and it is not until the sixth meeting, held on 21st March, 1884, that the word first appears in the minutes, as the title of a paper by Miss Caroline Haddon: "The Two Socialisms"; to which is appended a note in the handwriting of Sydney Olivier: "This paper is stated to have been devoted to a comparison between the Socialism of the Fabian Society and that of the S.D.F." The Society, in fact, began its career with that disregard of mere names which has always distinguished it. The resolutions already recorded, advocating the reconstruction of society on a non-competitive basis with the object of remedying the evils of poverty, embody the essence of Socialism, and our first publication, Tract No. 1, was so thorough-going a statement of Socialism that it has been kept in print ever since. But neither in Tract No. 1 nor in Tract No. 2 does the word Socialism occur, and it is not till Tract No. 3, published in June, 1885, that we find the words "the Fabian Society having in view the advance of Socialism in England." At this stage it is clear that the Society was socialist without recognising itself as part of a world-wide movement, and it was only subsequently that it adopted the word which alone adequately expressed its ideas.

At the second meeting, on 25th January, 1884, reports were presented on a lecture by Henry George and a Conference of the Democratic Federation (later the Social Democratic Federation); the rules were adopted, and Mr. J.G. Stapleton read a paper on "Social conditions in England with a view to social reconstruction or development." This was the first of the long series of Fabian fortnightly lectures which have been continued ever since. On February 29th, after a paper on the Democratic Federation, Mr. Bland moved: "That whilst not entirely agreeing with the statements and phrases used in the pamphlets of the Democratic Federation, and in the speeches of Mr. Hyndman, this Society considers that the Democratic Federation is doing good and useful work and is worthy of sympathy and support." This was carried nem. con. On March 7th a pamphlet committee was nominated, and on March 21st the Executive was reappointed. On April 4th the Pamphlet Committee reported, and 2000 copies of "Fabian Tract No. 1" were ordered to be printed.

This four-page leaflet has now remained in print for over thirty years, and there is no reason to suppose that the demand for it will soon cease. According to tradition, it was drafted by W.L. Phillips, a house-painter, at that time the only "genuine working man" in our ranks. He had been introduced to me by a Positivist friend, and was in his way a remarkable man, ready at any time to talk of his experiences of liberating slaves by the "Underground Railway" in the United States. He worked with us cordially for several years and then gradually dropped out. The original edition of "Why are the many poor?" differs very little from that now in circulation. It was revised some years later by Bernard Shaw, who cut down the rhetoric and sharpened the phraseology, but the substance has not been changed. It is remarkable as containing a sneer at Christianity, the only one to be found in the publications of the Society. Perhaps this was a rebound from excess of "subordination of material things to spiritual things" insisted on by the Fellowship of the New Life!

The tract had on its title page two mottoes, the second of which has played some part in the Society's history. They were produced, again according to tradition, by Frank Podmore, and, though printed as quotations, are not to be discovered in any history:

"Wherefore it may not be gainsaid that the fruit of this man's long taking of counsel — and (by the many so deemed) untimeous delays — was the safe-holding for all men, his fellow-citizens, of the Common Weal."

"For the right moment you must wait, as Fabius did most patiently, when warring against Hannibal, though many censured his delays; but when the time comes you must strike hard, as Fabius did, or your waiting will be in vain, and fruitless."

It has been pointed out by Mr. H.G. Wells, and by others before him, that Fabius never did strike hard; and many have enquired when the right time for the Fabians to strike would come. In fact, we recognised at that time that we did not know what were the remedies for the evils of society as we saw them and that the right time for striking would not come until we knew where to strike. Taken together as the two mottoes were first printed, this meaning is obvious. The delay was to be for the purpose of "taking counsel."

Tract No. 1, excellent as it is, shows a sense of the evil, but gives no indication of the remedy. Its contents are commonplace, and in no sense characteristic of the Society. The men who were to make its reputation had not yet found it out, and at this stage our chief characteristic was a lack of self-confidence unusual amongst revolutionaries. We had with considerable courage set out to reconstruct society, and we frankly confessed that we did not know how to go about it.

The next meeting to which we need refer took place on May 16th. The minutes merely record that Mr. Rowland Estcourt read a paper on "The Figures of Mr. Mallock," but a pencil note in the well-known handwriting of Bernard Shaw has been subsequently added: "This meeting was made memorable by the first appearance of Bernard Shaw."

On September 5th Bernard Shaw was elected a member, and at the following meeting on September 19th his first contribution to the literature of the Society, Pamphlet No. 2, was read. The influence of his intellectual outlook was immediate, and already the era of "highest moral possibilities" seems remote. Tract No. 2 was never reprinted and the number of copies in existence outside public libraries is small: it is therefore worth reproducing in full.

THE FABIAN SOCIETY

17 Osnaburgh Street, Regent's Park Fabian Tract No. 2

A MANIFESTO

"For always in thine eyes, O liberty, Shines that high light whereby the world is saved; And though thou slay us, we will trust in thee."

London: George Standring, 8 & 9 Finsbury Street, E.C. 1884.

A MANIFESTO

THE FABIANS are associated for spreading the following opinions held by them and discussing their practical consequences.

That under existing circumstances wealth cannot be enjoyed without dishonour or foregone without misery.

That it is the duty of each member of the State to provide for his or her wants by his or her own Labour.

That a life interest in the Land and Capital of the nation is the birthright of every individual born within its confines and that access to this birthright should not depend upon the will of any private person other than the person seeking it.

That the most striking result of our present system of farming out the national Land and Capital to private persons has been the division of Society into hostile classes, with large appetites and no dinners at one extreme and large dinners and no appetites at the other.

That the practice of entrusting the Land of the nation to private persons in the hope that they will make the best of it has been discredited by the consistency with which they have made the worst of it; and that Nationalisation of the Land in some form is a public duty.

That the pretensions of Capitalism to encourage Invention and to distribute its benefits in the fairest way attainable, have been discredited by the experience of the nineteenth century.

That, under the existing system of leaving the National Industry to organise itself Competition has the effect of rendering adulteration, dishonest dealing and inhumanity compulsory.

That since Competition amongst producers admittedly secures to the public the most satisfactory products, the State should compete with all its might in every department of production.

That such restraints upon Free Competition as the penalties for infringing the Postal monopoly, and the withdrawal of workhouse and prison labour from the markets, should be abolished.

That no branch of Industry should be carried on at a profit by the central administration.

That the Public Revenue should be levied by a direct Tax; and that the central administration should have no legal power to hold back for the replenishment of the Public Treasury any portion of the proceeds of Industries administered by them.

That the State should compete with private individuals—especially with parents—in providing happy homes for children, so that every child may have a refuge from the tyranny or neglect of its natural custodians.

That Men no longer need special political privileges to protect them against Women, and that the sexes should henceforth enjoy equal political rights.

That no individual should enjoy any Privilege in consideration of services rendered to the State by his or her parents or other relations.

That the State should secure a liberal education and an equal share in the National Industry to each of its units.

That the established Government has no more right to call itself the State than the smoke of London has to call itself the weather.

That we had rather face a Civil War than such another century of suffering as the present one has been."

It would be easy in the light of thirty years' experience to write at much length on these propositions. They are, of course, unqualified "Shaw." The minutes state that each was discussed and separately adopted. Three propositions, the nature of which is not recorded, were at a second meeting rejected, while the proposition on heredity was drafted and inserted by order of the meeting. I recollect demurring to the last proposition, and being assured by the author that it was all right since in fact no such alternative would ever be offered!

The persistency of Mr. Shaw's social philosophy is remarkable. His latest volume deals with parents and children, the theme he touched on in 1884; his social ideal is still a birthright life interest in national wealth, and "an equal share in national industry," the latter a phrase more suggestive than lucid. On the other hand, he, like the rest of us, was then by no means clear as to the distinction between Anarchism and Socialism. The old Radical prejudice in favour of direct taxation, so that the State may never handle a penny not wrung from the reluctant and acutely conscious taxpayer, the doctrinaire objection to State monopolies, and the modern view that municipal enterprises had better be carried on at cost price, are somewhat inconsistently commingled with the advocacy of universal State competition in industry. It may further be noticed that we were as yet unconscious of the claims and aims of the working people. Our Manifesto covered a wide field, but it nowhere touches Co-operation or Trade Unionism, wages or hours of labour. We were still playing with abstractions, Land and Capital, Industry and Competition, the Individual and the State.

In connection with the first tracts another point may be mentioned. The Society has stuck to the format adopted in these early days, and with a few special exceptions all its publications have been issued in the same style, and with numbers running on consecutively. For all sorts of purposes the advantage of this continuity has been great.

On January 2nd, 1885, Bernard Shaw was elected to the Executive Committee, and about the same time references to the Industrial Remuneration Conference appear in the minutes. This remarkable gathering, made possible by a gift of £1000 from Mr. Miller of Edinburgh, was summoned to spend three days in discussing the question, "Has the increase of products of industry within the last hundred years tended most to the benefit of capitalists and employers or to that of the working classes, whether artisans, labourers or others? And in what relative proportions in any given period?"

The second day was devoted to "Remedies," and the third to the question, "Would the more general distribution of capital or land or the State management of capital or land promote or impair the production of wealth and the welfare of the community?" The Fabian Society appointed two delegates, J.G. Stapleton and Hubert Bland, but Bernard Shaw apparently took the place of the latter.

It met on January 28th, at the Prince's Hall, Piccadilly. Mr. Arthur J. Balfour read a paper in which he made an observation worth recording: "As will be readily believed, I am no Socialist, but to compare the work of such men as Mr. (Henry) George with that of such men, for instance, as Karl Marx, either in respect of its intellectual force, its consistency, its command of reasoning in general, or of economic reasoning in particular, seems to me absurd."

The Conference was the first occasion in which the Fabian Society emerged from its drawing-room obscurity, and the speech of Bernard Shaw on the third day was probably the first he delivered before an audience of more than local importance. One passage made an impression on his friends and probably on the public. "It was," he said, "the desire of the President that nothing should be said that might give pain to particular classes. He was about to refer to a modern class, the burglars, but if there was a burglar present he begged him to believe that he cast no reflection upon his profession, and that he was not unmindful of his great skill and enterprise: his risks—so much greater than those of the most speculative capitalist, extending as they did to risk of liberty and life—his abstinence; or finally of the great number of people to whom he gave employment, including criminal attorneys, policemen, turnkeys, builders of gaols, and it might be the hangman. He did not wish to hurt the feelings of shareholders ... or of landlords ... any more than he wished to pain burglars. He would merely point out that all three inflicted on the community an injury of precisely the same nature."

It may be added that Mr. Shaw was patted on the back by a subsequent speaker, Mr. John Wilson, of the Durham Miners, for many years M.P. for Mid-Durham, and by no means an habitual supporter of Socialists.

The stout volume in which the proceedings are published is now but seldom referred to, but it is a somewhat significant record of the intellectual unrest of the period, an indication that the governing classes even at this early date in the history of English Socialism, were prepared to consider its claims, and to give its proposals a respectful hearing.

The early debates in the Society were in the main on things abstract or Utopian. Social Reconstruction was a constant theme, Hubert Bland outlined "Revolutionary Prospects" in January, 1885, and Bernard Shaw in February combated "The Proposed Abolition of the Currency."

On March 6th a new departure began: a Committee was appointed to collect "facts concerning the working of the Poor Law," with special reference to alleged official attempts to disprove "great distress amongst the workers." It does not appear that the Report was ever completed.

On March 20th Sidney Webb read a paper on "The Way Out," and on the 1st May he was elected a member along with his Colonial Office colleague Sydney Olivier. On May 15th is recorded the election of Harold Cox, subsequently M.P., and now editor of the "Edinburgh Review."

The Society was now finding its feet. On April 17th it had been resolved to send a delegate "to examine into and report upon the South Yorkshire Miners"! And on the same day it was determined to get up a Soirée. This gathering, held in Gower Street, was memorable because it was attended by Mrs. Annie Besant, then notorious as an advocate of Atheism and Malthusianism, the heroine of several famous law cases, and a friend and colleague of Charles Bradlaugh. Mrs. Besant was elected a member a few weeks later, and she completed the list of the seven who subsequently wrote "Fabian Essays," with the exception of Graham Wallas, who did not join the Society until April, 1886.

But although Sidney Webb had become a Fabian the scientific spirit was not yet predominant. Bernard Shaw had, then as now, a strong objection to the peasant agriculture of his native land, and he submitted to the Society a characteristic leaflet addressed: "To provident Landlords and Capitalists, a suggestion and a warning." "The Fabian Society," it says, "having in view the advance of Socialism and the threatened subversion of the powers hitherto exercised by private proprietors of the national land and capital ventures plainly to warn all such proprietors that the establishment of Socialism in England means nothing less than the compulsion of all members of the upper class, without regard to sex or condition, to work for their own living." The tract, which is a very brief one, goes on to recommend the proprietary classes to "support all undertakings having for their object the parcelling out of waste or inferior lands amongst the labouring class" for sundry plausible reasons. At the foot of the title page, in the smallest of type, is the following: "Note — Great care should be taken to keep this tract out of the hands of radical workmen, Socialist demagogues and the like, as they are but too apt to conclude that schemes favourable to landlords cannot be permanently advantageous to the working class." This elaborate joke was, except for one amendment, adopted as drafted on June 5th, 1885, and there is a tradition that it was favourably reviewed by a Conservative newspaper!

The Society still met as a rule at 17 Osnaburgh Street, or in the rooms of Frank Podmore at 14 Dean's Yard, Westminster, but it was steadily growing and new members were elected at every meeting. Although most of the members were young men of university education, the Society included people of various ages. To us at any rate Mrs. James Hinton, widow of Dr. Hinton, and her sisters, Miss Haddon and Miss Caroline Haddon, seemed to be at least elderly. Mrs. Robins, her husband (a successful architect), and her daughter, who acted as "assistant" honorary secretary for the first eighteen months, lent an air of prosperous respectability to our earliest meetings. Mr. and Mrs. J. Glode Stapleton, who were prominent members for some years, were remarkable amongst us because they drove to our meetings in their own brougham! The working classes, as before mentioned, had but a single representative. Another prominent member at this period was Mrs. Charlotte M. Wilson, wife of a stock-broker living in Hampstead, who a short time later "simplified" into a cottage at the end of the Heath, called Wildwood

Farm, now a part of the Garden Suburb Estate, where Fabians for many years held the most delightful of their social gatherings. Mrs. Wilson was elected to the Executive of five in December, 1884 (Mrs. Wilson, H. Bland, E.R. Pease, G. Bernard Shaw and F. Keddell), but after some time devoted herself entirely to the Anarchist movement, led by Prince Kropotkin, and for some years edited their paper, "Freedom." But she remained throughout a member of the Fabian Society, and twenty years later she resumed her Fabian activity, as will be related in a later chapter.

All this time the Socialist movement in England was coming into public notice with startling rapidity. In January, 1884, "Justice, the organ of the Democratic Federation," was founded, and in August of that year the Federation made the first of its many changes of name, and became the Social Democratic Federation or S.D.F. The public then believed, as the Socialists also necessarily believed, that Socialism would be so attractive to working-class electors that they would follow its banner as soon as it was raised, and the candidatures undertaken by the S.D.F. at the General Election in November, 1885, produced widespread alarm amongst politicians of both parties. The following account of this episode from Fabian Tract 41, "The Early History of the Fabian Society," was written by Bernard Shaw in 1892, and describes the events and our attitude at the time far more freshly and graphically than anything I can write nearly thirty years later.

After explaining why he preferred joining the Fabian Society rather than the S.D.F., Mr. Shaw goes on (pp. 4-7):

> "However, as I have said, in 1885 our differences [from other Socialists] were latent or instinctive; and we denounced the capitalists as thieves at the Industrial Remuneration Conference, and, among ourselves, talked revolution, anarchism, labour notes *versus* pass-books, and all the rest of it, on the tacit assumption that the object of our campaign, with its watchwords, *'educate, agitate, organize,'* was to bring about a tremendous smash-up of existing society, to be succeeded by complete Socialism. And this meant that we had no true practical understanding either of existing society or Socialism. Without being quite definitely aware of this, we yet felt it to a certain extent all along; for it was at this period that we contracted the invaluable habit of freely laughing at ourselves which has always distinguished us, and which has saved us from becoming hampered by the gushing

enthusiasts who mistake their own emotions for public movements. From the first, such people fled after one glance at us, declaring that we were not serious. Our preference for practical suggestions and criticisms, and our impatience of all general expressions of sympathy with working-class aspirations, not to mention our way of chaffing our opponents in preference to denouncing them as enemies of the human race, repelled from us some warm-hearted and eloquent Socialists, to whom it seemed callous and cynical to be even commonly self-possessed in the presence of the sufferings upon which Socialists make war. But there was far too much equality and personal intimacy among the Fabians to allow of any member presuming to get up and preach at the rest in the fashion which the working-classes still tolerate submissively from their leaders. We knew that a certain sort of oratory was useful for 'stoking up' public meetings; but we needed no stoking up, and, when any orator tried the process on us, soon made him understand that he was wasting his time and ours. I, for one, should be very sorry to lower the intellectual standard of the Fabian by making the atmosphere of its public discussions the least bit more congenial to stale declamation than it is at present. If our debates are to be kept wholesome, they cannot be too irreverent or too critical. And the irreverence, which has become traditional with us, comes down from those early days when we often talked such nonsense that we could not help laughing at ourselves.

Tory Gold At The 1885 Election.

When I add that in 1885 we had only 40 members, you will be able to form a sufficient notion of the Fabian Society in its nonage. In that year there occurred an event which developed the latent differences between ourselves and the Social-Democratic Federation. The Federation said then, as it still says, that its policy is founded on a recognition of the existence of a Class War. How far the fact of the working classes being at war with the proprietary classes justifies them in suspending the observance of the ordinary social obligations in dealing with them was never settled; but at that time we were decidedly less scrupulous than we are now in our ideas on the subject; and we all said freely that as gunpowder destroyed the feudal system, so the capitalist system could not long survive the invention of dynamite. Not that we are dynamitards: indeed the absurdity of the inference shows how innocent we were of any practical acquaintance with explosives; but we thought that the statement about gunpowder and feudalism was historically true, and that it would do the capitalists good to remind them of it. Suddenly, however, the Federation made a very startling practical application of the Class War doctrine. They did not blow anybody up; but in the general election of 1885 they ran two candidates in London—Mr. Williams, in Hampstead, who got 27 votes, and Mr. Fielding, in Kennington, who got 32 votes. And they made no secret of the fact that the expenses of these elections had been paid by one of the established political parties in order to split the vote of the other. From the point of view of the abstract moralist there was nothing to be said against the transaction; since it was evident that Socialist statesmanship must for a long time to come consist largely of taking advantage of the party dissensions between the Unsocialists. It may easily happen to-morrow that the Liberal party may offer to contribute to the expenses of a Fabian candidate in a hopelessly Tory stronghold, in order to substantiate its pretensions to encourage Labour representation. Under such circumstances it is quite possible that we may say to the Fabian in question, Accept by all means; and deliver propagandist addresses all over the place. Suppose that the Liberal party offers to bear part of Mr. Sidney Webb's expenses at the forthcoming County Council election at Deptford, as they undoubtedly will, by means of the usual National Liberal Club subscription, in the case of the poorer Labour candidates. Mr. Webb, as a matter of personal preference for an independence which he is fortunately able to afford, will refuse. But suppose Mr. Webb were not in that fortunate position, as some Labour candidates will not be! It is quite certain that not the smallest odium would attach to the acceptance of a Liberal grant-in-aid. Now the idea that taking Tory money is worse than taking Liberal money is clearly a Liberal party idea and not a Social-Democratic one.

In 1885 there was not the slightest excuse for regarding the Tory party as any more hostile to Socialism than the Liberal party; and Mr. Hyndman's classical quotation,'Non olet' — 'It does not smell,' meaning that there is no difference in the flavour of Tory and Whig gold once it comes into the Socialist treasury, was a sufficient retort to the accusations of moral corruption which were levelled at him. But the Tory money job, as it was called, was none the less a huge mistake in tactics. Before it took place, the Federation loomed large in the imagination of the public and the political parties. This is conclusively proved by the fact that the Tories thought that the Socialists could take enough votes from the Liberals to make it worth while to pay the expenses of two Socialist candidates in London. The day after the election everyone knew that the Socialists were an absolutely negligeable quantity there as far as voting power was concerned. They had presented the Tory party with 57 votes, at a cost of about £8 apiece. What was worse, they had shocked London Radicalism, to which Tory money was an utter abomination. It is hard to say which cut the more foolish figure, the Tories who had spent their money for nothing, or the Socialists who had sacrificed their reputation for worse than nothing.

"The disaster was so obvious that there was an immediate falling off from the Federation, on the one hand of the sane tacticians of the movement, and on the other of those out-and-out Insurrectionists who repudiated political action altogether, and were only too glad to be able to point to a discreditable instance of it. Two resolutions were passed, one by the Socialist League and the other by the Fabian Society. Here is the Fabian resolution:

"'That the conduct of the Council of the Social-Democratic Federation in accepting money from the Tory party in payment of the election expenses of Socialist candidates is calculated to disgrace the Socialist movement in England,'- 4th Dec., 1885."

The result of this resolution, passed by 15 votes to 4, was the first of the very few splits which are recorded in the history of the Society. Frederick Keddell, the first honorary secretary, resigned and I took his place, whilst a few weeks later Sidney Webb was elected to the vacancy on the Executive.

In 1886 Socialism was prominently before the public. Unemployment reached a height which has never since been touched. Messrs. Hyndman, Champion, Burns, and Williams were actually tried for sedition, but happily acquitted; and public opinion was justified in regarding Socialism rather as destructive and disorderly than as constructive, and, as is now often said, even too favourable to repressive legislation. In these commotions the Society as a whole took no part, and its public activities were limited to a meeting at South Place Chapel, on December 18th, 1885, addressed by Mrs. Besant.

In March, 1886, the Executive Committee was increased to seven by the addition of Mrs. Besant and Frank Podmore, and in April Tract No. 4, "What Socialism Is," was approved for publication. It begins with a historical preface, touching on the Wars of the Roses, Tudor confiscation of land, the enclosure of commons, the Industrial Revolution, and so on. Surplus value and the tendency of wages to a minimum are mentioned, and the valuable work of Trade Unionism—sometimes regarded by Guild Socialists and others nowadays as a recent discovery—is alluded to: indeed the modern syndicalist doctrine was anticipated: the workman, it is said, "has been forced to sell himself for a mess of pottage and is consequently deprived of the guidance of his own life and the direction of his own labour." Socialist opinion abroad, it says, "has taken shape in two distinct schools, Collectivist and Anarchist. English Socialism is not yet Anarchist or Collectivist, not yet definite enough in point of policy to be classified. There is a mass of Socialist feeling not yet conscious of itself as Socialism. But when the conscious Socialists of England discover their position they also will probably fall into two parties: a Collectivist party supporting a strong central administration, and a counterbalancing Anarchist party defending individual initiative against that administration. In some such fashion progress and stability will probably be secured under Socialism by the conflict of the uneradicable Tory and Whig instincts in human nature."

It will be noticed that even in this period of turmoil the Society was altogether constitutional in its outlook; political parties of Socialists and Anarchists combining progress with stability were the features of the future we foresaw.

By this time the Society was thoroughly aware of its relation to international socialism, and the remaining six pages of the tract are occupied by expositions of the alternatives above alluded to. "Collectivism" is summarised from Bebel's "Woman in the Past, Present, and Future," and is a somewhat mechanical scheme of executive committees in each local commune or district representing each branch of industry, elected by universal suffrage for brief periods of office and paid at the rate of ordinary workmen; and of a central Executive Committee chosen in like manner or else directly appointed by the local Communal Councils. The second part consists of "Anarchism, drawn up by C.M. Wilson on behalf of the London Anarchists." This is a statement of abstract principles which frankly admits that "Anarchists have no fears that in discarding the Collectivist dream of the scientific regulation of industry and inventing no formulas for social conditions as yet unrealised, they are neglecting the essential for the visionary."

This tract was never reprinted, and, of course, it attracted no attention. It was however the first of the long series of Fabian tracts that aimed at supplying information and thus carrying out the original object of the Society, the education of its members and the systematic study of the reconstruction of the social system.

The spring of 1886 was occupied with arrangements for the Conference, which was held at South Place Chapel on June 9th, 10th, and 11th.

Here again a quotation from Bernard Shaw's *Early History of the Fabian Society* is the best description available:

> "The Fabian Conference Of 1886.
>
> "You will now ask to be told what the Fabians had been doing all this time. Well, I think it must be admitted that we were overlooked in the excitements of the unemployed agitation, which had, moreover, caused the Tory money affair to be forgotten. The Fabians were disgracefully backward in open-air speaking. Up to quite a recent date, Graham Wallas, myself, and Mrs. Besant were the only representative open-air speakers in the Society, whereas the Federation speakers, Burns, Hyndman, Andrew Hall, Tom Mann, Champion, Burrows, with the Socialist Leaguers, were at it constantly. On the whole, the Church Parades and the rest were not in our line; and we were not wanted by the

men who were organizing them. Our only contribution to the agitation was a report which we printed in 1886, which recommended experiments in tobacco culture, and even hinted at compulsory military service, as means of absorbing some of the unskilled unemployed, but which went carefully into the practical conditions of relief works. Indeed, we are at present trying to produce a new tract on the subject without finding ourselves able to improve very materially on the old one in this respect. It was drawn up by Bland, Hughes, Podmore, Stapleton, and Webb, and was the first of our publications that contained any solid information. Its tone, however, was moderate and its style somewhat conventional; and the Society was still in so hot a temper on the social question that we refused to adopt it as a regular Fabian tract, and only issued it as a report printed for the information of members. Nevertheless we were coming to our senses rapidly by this time. We signalized our repudiation of political sectarianism in June, 1886, by inviting the Radicals, the Secularists, and anyone else who would come, to a great conference, modelled upon the Industrial Remuneration Conference, and dealing with the Nationalization of Land and Capital. It fully established the fact that we had nothing immediately practical to impart to the Radicals and that they had nothing to impart to us. The proceedings were fully reported for us; but we never had the courage even to read the shorthand writer's report, which still remains in MS. Before I refreshed my memory on the subject the other day, I had a vague notion that the Conference cost a great deal of money; that it did no good whatever; that Mr. Bradlaugh made a speech; that Mrs. Fenwick Miller, who had nothing on earth to do with us, was in the chair during part of the proceedings; and that the most successful paper was by a strange gentleman whom we had taken on trust as a Socialist, but who turned out to be an enthusiast on the subject of building more harbours. I find, however, on looking up the facts, that no less than fifty-three societies sent delegates; that the guarantee fund for expenses was £100; and that the discussions were kept going for three afternoons and three evenings. The Federation boycotted us; but the 'Times' reported us. Eighteen papers were read, two of them by members of Parliament, and most of the rest by well-known people. William Morris and Dr. Aveling read papers as delegates from the Socialist League; the National Secular Society sent Mr. Foote and Mr. [John M.] Robertson, the latter contributing a 'Scheme of Taxation' in which he anticipated much of what was subsequently adopted as the Fabian program; Wordsworth Donisthorpe took the field for Anarchism of the type advocated by the authors of 'A Plea for Liberty'; Stewart Headlam spoke for Christian Socialism and the Guild of St. Matthew; Dr. Pankhurst dealt with the situation from the earlier Radical point of view; and various Socialist papers were read by Mrs. Besant, Sidney Webb, and Edward Carpenter, besides one by Stuart Glennie, who subsequently left us because we fought shy of the Marriage Question when revising our 'Basis.' I mention all this in order to show you how much more important this abortive Conference looked than the present one. Yet all that can be said for it is that it made us known to the Radical clubs and proved that we were able to manage a conference in a businesslike way. It also, by the way, showed off our pretty prospectus with the design by Crane at the top, our stylish-looking blood-red invitation cards, and the other little smartnesses on which we then prided ourselves. We used to be plentifully sneered at as fops and arm-chair Socialists for our attention to these details; but I think it was by no means the least of our merits that we always, as far as our means permitted, tried to make our printed documents as handsome as possible, and did our best to destroy the association between revolutionary literature and slovenly printing on paper that is nasty without being cheap. One effect of this was that we were supposed to be much richer than we really were, because we generally got better value and a finer show for our money than the other Socialist societies."

Three members of Parliament, Charles Bradlaugh, William Saunders, and Dr. G.B. Clark, took part. The Dr. Pankhurst mentioned was the husband of Mrs. Pankhurst, later the leader of the Women's Social and Political Union.

The reference in the foregoing passage to the report on "The Government Organisation of Unemployed Labour," prepared concurrently with the organisation of the Conference, is by no means adequate. The Report attracted but little attention at the time, even in the Society itself, but it is in fact the first typically Fabian publication, and the first in which Sidney Webb took part. Much subsequent experience has convinced me that whenever Webb is on a committee it may be assumed in default of positive evidence to the contrary that its report is his work. Webb however maintains that to the best of his recollection the work was shared between Podmore and himself, the simple arrangement being that Podmore wrote the first half and Webb the second. The tract is an attempt to deal with a pressing social problem on constructive lines. It surveys the field, analyses the phenomena presented, and suggests practicable remedies. It is however a very cautious document. Webb was then old as an economist, and very young as a Socialist; none of the rest of the Committee had the knowledge, if they had the will, to stand up to him. Therefore we find snippets from the theory of economic "balance" which was universally regarded as valid in those days.

"In practice the government obtains its technical skill by attracting men from other employers, and its capital in a mobile form by attracting it from other possessors. It gets loans on the money market, which is thereby rendered more stringent; the rate of interest rises and the loans made to other borrowers are diminished."

But the particular interest of the Report at the present day is the fact that it contains the germs of many ideas which more than twenty years later formed the leading features of the Minority Report of the Poor Law Commission.

At that time it was universally believed that the slum dwellers of London were mainly recruited by rural immigrants, and this error — disproved several years later by the painstaking statistical investigations of Mr. (now Sir) H. Llewelyn Smith — vitiates much of the reasoning of the Report.

After analysing the causes of unemployment on lines now familiar to all, and denouncing private charity with vehemence worthy of the Charity Organisation Society, it recommends the revival of social life in our villages in order to keep the country people from crowding into the slums. The Dock Companies are urged to organise their casual labour into permanently employed brigades: and it is suggested, as in the "Minority Report," that "the most really 'remunerative' form of 'relief' works for the unemployed would often be a course of instruction in some new trade or handicraft." Technical education is strongly recommended; Labour Bureaux are advocated; State cultivation of tobacco is suggested as a means of employing labour on the land (private cultivation of tobacco was until recently prohibited by law), as well as municipal drink supply, State railways, and "universal military (home) service" as a means of promoting "the growth of social consciousness,"

The Report is unequal. An eloquent but irrelevant passage on the social effects of bringing the railway contractor's navvies to a rural village was possibly contributed by Hubert Bland, whilst the conclusion, a magniloquent eulogy of the moral value of Government service, written, according to Webb's recollection, by Frank Podmore, is evidently the work of a civil servant who has not got over the untamed enthusiasms of youth!

The Report shows immature judgment, but also in parts remarkable foresight, and a complete realisation of the right scientific method. With State tobacco farms and the public organisation of a corps of peripatetic State navvies, the childhood stage of the Fabian Society may be said to conclude.

My own connection with the Society also changed. In the spring of 1886 I gave up my business on the Stock Exchange and in the summer went to Newcastle-on-Tyne, where I lived till the autumn of 1890. My account of the Society for the next three years is therefore in the main derived from its records. Sydney Olivier succeeded me as "Acting Secretary," but for some months I was still nominally the secretary, a fact of much significance to my future, since it enabled me if I liked to deal with correspondence, and it was through a letter to the secretary of the Society, answered by me from Newcastle, that I made the acquaintance of the lady who three years later became my wife.

Chapter IV   The Formation of Fabian Policy: 1886-9

The factors of success; priority of date; the men who made it – The controversy over policy – The Fabian Parliamentary League – "Facts for Socialists" – The adoption of the Basis – The seven Essayists in command – Lord Haldane – The "Essays" as lectures – How to train for Public Life – Fabians on the London School Board – "Facts for Londoners" – Municipal Socialism – "The Eight Hours Bill"

The Society was now fully constituted, and for the next three years its destiny was controlled by the seven who subsequently wrote "Fabian Essays." But it was still a very small and quite obscure body. Mrs. Besant, alone of its leaders, was known beyond its circle, and at that period few outside the working classes regarded her with respect. The Society still met, as a rule, at the house of one or other of the members, and to the founders, who numbered about 20, only about 67 members had been added by June, 1886. The receipts for the year to March, 1886, were no more than £35 19s., but as the expenditure only amounted to £27 6s. 6d., the Society had already adopted its lifelong habit of paying its way punctually, though it must be confessed that a complaisant printer and a series of lucky windfalls have contributed to that result.

The future success of the Society was dependent in the main on two factors then already in existence. The first was its foundation before there was any other definitely Socialist body in England. The

Social Democratic Federation did not adopt that name until August, 1884; the Fabian Society can therefore claim technical priority, and consequently it has never had to seek acceptance by the rest of the Socialist movement. At any later date it would have been impossible for a relatively small middle-class society to obtain recognition as an acknowledged member of the Socialist confraternity. We were thus in a position to welcome the formation of working-class Socialist societies, but it is certain that in the early days they would never have welcomed us.

Regret has been sometimes expressed, chiefly by foreign observers, that the Society has maintained its separate identity. Why, it has been asked, did not the middle-class leaders of the Society devote their abilities directly to aiding the popular organisations, instead of "keeping themselves to themselves" like ultra-respectable suburbans?

If this had been possible I am convinced that the loss would have exceeded the gain, but in the early years it was not possible. The Social Democrats of those days asserted that unquestioning belief in every dogma attributed to Marx was essential to social salvation, and that its only way was revolution, by which they meant, not the complete transformation of society, but its transformation by means of rifles and barricades; they were convinced that a successful repetition of the Commune of Paris was the only method by which their policy could prevail. The Fabians realised from the first that no such revolution was likely to take place, and that constant talk about it was the worst possible way to commend Socialism to the British working class. And indeed a few years later it was necessary to establish a new working-class Socialist Society, the Independent Labour Party, in order to get clear both of the tradition of revolutionary violence and of the vain repetition of Marxian formulas. If the smaller society had merged itself in the popular movement, its criticism, necessary, as it proved to be, to the success of Socialism in England, would have been voted down, and its critics either silenced or expelled. Of this criticism I shall have more to say in another place.

But there was another reason why this course would have been impracticable. The Fabians were not suited either by ability, temperament, or conditions to be leaders of a popular revolutionary party. Mrs. Besant with her gift of splendid oratory and her long experience of agitation was an exception, but her connection with the movement lasted no more than five years. Of the others Shaw did not and does not now possess that unquestioning faith in recognised principles which is the stock-in-trade of political leadership: and whilst Webb might have been a first-class minister at the head of a department, his abilities would have been wasted as a leader in a minority. But there was a more practical bar. The Fabians were mostly civil servants or clerks in private employ. The methods of agitation congenial to them were compatible with their occupations: those of the Social Democrats were not. Indeed in those days no question of amalgamation was ever mooted.

But it must be remembered by critics that so far as concerns the Fabian Society, the absence of identity in organisation has never led to such hostility as has been common amongst Continental Socialists. Since the vote of censure in relation to the "Tory Gold," the Fabian Society has never interfered with the doings of its friendly rivals. The two Societies have occasionally co-operated, but as a rule they have severally carried on their own work, each recognising the value of many of the activities of the other, and on the whole confining mutual criticism within reasonable limits.

The second and chief reason for the success of the Society was its good fortune in attaching to its service a group of young men, then altogether unknown, whose reputation has gradually spread, in two or three cases, all over the world, and who have always been in the main identified with Fabianism. Very rarely in the history of voluntary organisations has a group of such exceptional people come together almost accidentally and worked unitedly together for so many years for the furtherance of the principles in which they believed. Others have assisted according to their abilities and opportunities, but to the Fabian Essayists belongs the credit of creating the Fabian Society.

For several years, and those perhaps the most important in the history of the Society, the period, in fact, of adolescence, the Society was governed by the seven Essayists, and chiefly by four or five of them. Mrs. Besant had made her reputation in other fields, and belonged, in a sense, to an earlier generation; she was unrivalled as an expositor and an agitator, and naturally preferred the work that she did best. William Clarke, also, was just a little of an outsider: he attended committees irregularly, and although he did what he was persuaded to do with remarkable force — he was an admirable lecturer and an efficient journalist — he had no initiative. He was solitary in his habits, and in his latter years, overshadowed by ill-health, he became almost morose. Hubert Bland, again, was always something of a critic. He was a Tory by instinct wherever he was not a Socialist, and whilst thoroughly united with the others for all purposes of the Society, he lived the rest of his life apart. But the other four Essayists, Sidney Webb, Bernard Shaw, Graham Wallas, and Sydney Olivier, then and for many years afterwards may be said to have worked and thought together in an intellectual partnership. Webb and Olivier were colleagues in the Colonial Office, and it is said that for some time the Fabian records — they were not very bulky — were stored on a table in Downing Street. For many years there were probably few evenings of the week and few holidays which two or more of them did not spend together.

In 1885 or early in 1886 a group which included those four and many others formed a reading society for the discussion of Marx's "Capital." The meetings — I attended them until I left London — were held in Hampstead, sometimes at the house of Mrs. Gilchrist, widow of the biographer of Blake, sometimes at that of Mrs. C.M. Wilson, and finally at the Hampstead Public Library. Later on the Society was called "The Hampstead Historic," and its discussions, which continued for several years, had much to do with settling the Fabian attitude towards Marxian economics and historical theory.

It was this exceptional group of leaders, all intimate friends, all loyal to each other, and to the cause they were associated to advocate, and all far above the average in vigour and ability, that in a few years turned an obscure drawing-room society into a factor in national politics.

At the meeting on June 19th, 1886, at 94 Cornwall Gardens, Sydney Olivier assumed the duties of Secretary, and the minutes began to be written with less formality than before. It is recorded that "Graham Wallas read a paper on Personal Duty under the present system. A number of questions from Fabians more or less in trouble about their souls were answered *ex cathedra* by Mr. Wallas, after which the Society was given to understand by G.B. Shaw that Joseph the Fifth Monarchy Man could show them a more excellent way. Joseph addressed the meeting for five minutes, on the subject of a community about to be established in British North America under the presidency of the Son of God. Sidney Webb, G. Bernard Shaw,

Annie Besant, [the Rev.] C.L. Marson and Adolph Smith discussed the subject of the paper with especial reference to the question of buying cheap goods and of the employment of the surplus income of pensioners, after which Graham Wallas replied and the meeting dispersed,"

William Morris lectured on "The Aims of Art" on July 2nd, at a public meeting at South Place Chapel, with Walter Crane in the chair; and Belfort Bax was the lecturer on July 17th.

The first meeting after the holidays was a memorable one, and a few words of introduction are necessary.

In normal times it may be taken for granted that in addition to the Government and the Opposition there is at least one party of Rebels. Generally there are more, since each section has its own rebels, down to the tiniest. In the eighties the rebels were Communist Anarchists, and to us at any rate they seemed more portentous than the mixed crowd of suffragettes and gentlemen from Oxford who before the war seemed to be leading the syndicalist rebels. Anarchist Communism was at any rate a consistent and almost sublime doctrine. Its leaders, such as Prince Kropotkin and Nicholas Tchaykovsky, were men of outstanding ability and unimpeachable character, and the rank and file, mostly refugees from European oppression, had direct relations with similar parties abroad, the exact extent and significance of which we could not calculate.

The Socialist League, founded in 1885 by William Morris, Dr. Edward Aveling, and others, as the result of a quarrel, mainly personal, with the leaders of the Social Democrats, soon developed its own doctrine, and whilst never until near its dissolution definitely anarchist, it was always dominated by the artistic and anti-political temperament of Morris. Politically the Fabians were closer to the Social Democrats, but their hard dogmatism was repellent, whilst Morris had perhaps the most sympathetic and attractive personality of his day.

The crisis of the Society's policy is described in the following passage from Shaw's *Early History,*:

"By 1886 we had already found that we were of one mind as to the advisability of setting to work by the ordinary political methods and having done with Anarchism and vague exhortations to Emancipate the Workers. We had several hot debates on the subject with a section of the Socialist League which called itself Anti-State Communist, a name invented by Mr. Joseph Lane of that body. William Morris, who was really a free democrat of the Kropotkin type, backed up Lane, and went for us tooth and nail. Records of our warfare may be found in the volumes of the extinct magazine called 'To-day,' which was then edited by Hubert Bland; and they are by no means bad reading. We soon began to see that at the debates the opposition to us came from members of the Socialist League, who were present only as visitors. The question was, how many followers had our one ascertained Anarchist, Mrs. Wilson, among the silent Fabians. Bland and Mrs. Besant brought this question to an issue on the 17th September, 1886, at a meeting in Anderton's Hotel, by respectively seconding and moving the following resolution:

"'That it is advisable that Socialists should organize themselves as a political party for the purpose of transferring into the hands of the whole working community full control over the soil and the means of production, as well as over the production and distribution of wealth.'

"To this a rider was moved by William Morris as follows:

"'But whereas the first duty of Socialists is to educate the people to understand what their present position is and what their future might be, and to keep the principle of Socialism steadily before them; and whereas no Parliamentary party can exist without compromise and concession, which would hinder that education and obscure those principles, it would be a false step for Socialists to attempt to take part in the Parliamentary contest.'

"I shall not attempt to describe the debate, in which Morris, Mrs. Wilson, Davis, and Tochatti did battle with Burns, Mrs. Besant, Bland, Shaw, Donald, and Rossiter: that is, with Fabian and S.D.F. combined. Suffice it to say that the minutes of the meeting close with the following significant note by the secretary:

"'Subsequently to the meeting, the secretary received notice from the manager of Anderton's Hotel that the Society could not be accommodated there for any further meetings.'

Everybody voted, whether Fabian or not; and Mrs. Besant and Bland carried their resolution by 47 to 19, Morris's rider being subsequently rejected by 40 to 27."

A short contemporary report written by Mrs. Besant was published in "To-day" for October, 1886, from which it appears that "Invitations were sent out to all Socialist bodies in London," and that the irregularity of the proceedings alluded to by Shaw was intentional. The minutes of the proceedings treat the meeting as in ordinary course, but it is plain from Mrs. Besant's report that it was an informal attempt to clear the air in the Socialist movement as well as in the Society itself.

In order to avoid a breach with Mrs. Wilson and her Fabian sympathisers, it was resolved to form a Fabian Parliamentary League, which Fabians could join or not as they pleased; its constitution, dated February, 1887, is given in full in Tract No. 41; here it is only necessary to quote one passage which describes the policy of the League and of the Society, a policy of deliberate possibilism:

"The League will take active part in all general and local elections. Until a fitting opportunity arises for putting forward Socialist candidates to form the nucleus of a Socialist party in Parliament, it will confine itself to supporting those candidates who will go furthest in the direction of Socialism. It will not ally itself absolutely with any political party; it will jealously avoid being made use of for party purposes; and it will be guided in its action by the character, record, and pledges of the candidates before the constituencies. In Municipal, School Board, Vestry, and other local elections, the League will, as it finds itself strong enough, run candidates of its own, and by placing trustworthy Socialists on local representative bodies it will endeavour to secure the recognition of the Socialist principle in all the details of local government."

Its history is narrated in the same Tract:

"Here you have the first sketch of the Fabian policy of to-day. The Parliamentary League, however, was a short-lived affair. Mrs. Wilson's followers faded away, either by getting converted or leaving us. Indeed, it is a question with us to this day whether they did not owe their existence solely to our own imaginations. Anyhow, it soon became plain that the Society was solidly with the Executive on the subject of political action, and that there was no need for any separate organization at all. The League first faded into a Political Committee of the Society, and then merged silently and painlessly into the general body."

Amongst the lecturers of the autumn of 1886 were H.H. Champion on the Unemployed, Mrs. Besant on the Economic Position of Women, Percival Chubb, Bernard Shaw on "Socialism and the Family" — a pencil note in the minute book in the lecturer's handwriting says, "This was one of Shaw's most outrageous performances" — and, in the absence of the Rev. Stopford Brooke, another by Shaw on "Why we do not act up to our principles,"

A new Tract was adopted in January, 1887. No. 5, "Facts for Socialists," perhaps the most effective Socialist tract ever published in England. It has sold steadily ever since it was issued: every few years it has been revised and the figures brought up to date; the edition now on sale, published in 1915, is the eleventh. The idea was not new. Statistics of the distribution of our national income had been given, as previously mentioned, in one of the earliest manifestoes of the Democratic Federation. But in Tract 5 the exact facts were rubbed in with copious quotations from recognised authorities and illustrated by simple diagrams. The full title of the tract was "Facts for Socialists from the Political Economists and Statisticians," and the theme of it was to prove that every charge made by Socialism against the capitalist system could be justified by the writings of the foremost professors of economic science. It embodied another Fabian characteristic of considerable importance. Other Socialists then, and many Socialists now, endeavoured by all means to accentuate their differences from other people. Not content with forming societies to advocate their policy, they insisted that it was based on a science peculiar to themselves, the Marxian analysis of value, and the economic interpretation of history: they strove too to dissociate themselves from others by the adoption of peculiar modes of address — such as the use of the words "comrade" and "fraternal" — and they were so convinced that no good thing could come out of the Galilee of capitalism that any countenance of capitalist parties or of the capitalist press was deemed an act of treachery.

The Fabians, on the other hand, tended to the view that "we are all Socialists now." They held that the pronouncements of economic science must be either right or wrong, and in any case science was not a matter of party; they endeavoured to show that on their opponents' own principles they were logically compelled to be Socialists and must necessarily adopt Fabian solutions of social problems.

"Facts for Socialists" was the work of Sidney Webb. No other member possessed anything like his knowledge of economics and statistics. It is, as its title implies, simply a mass of quotations from standard works on Political Economy, strung together in order to prove that the bulk of the wealth annually produced goes to a small fraction of the community in return either for small services or for none at all, and that the poverty of the masses results, not as the individualists argue, from deficiencies of individual character, but, as John Stuart Mill had declared, from the excessive share of the national dividend that falls to the owners of land and capital.

After the settlement, by a compromise in structure, of the conflict between the anarchists and the collectivists, the Society entered a period of calm, and the Executive issued a circular complaining of the apathy of the members. Probably this is the first of the innumerable occasions on which it has been said that the Society had passed its prime. Moreover, the Executive Committee were blamed for "some habits" which had "a discouraging effect" on the rest of the Society, and it was resolved, for the first, but not the last time, to appoint a Committee to revise the Basis. The Committee consisted of the Executive and eight added members, amongst whom may be mentioned Walter Crane, the Rev. S.D. Headlam, and Graham Wallas. It is said that after many hours of discussion they arrived by compromise at an unanimous report, and that their draft was accepted by the Society without amendment. The report was presented to a meeting on June 3rd, 1887, of which I, on a visit to London, was chairman. It is unfortunate that the record of this meeting, at which the existing Basis of the Society was adopted, is the only one, in the whole history of the Society, which is incomplete. Possibly the colonial policy of the empire was disturbed, and the secretary occupied with exceptional official duties. Anyway the minutes were left unfinished in June, were continued in October, and were never completed or recorded as confirmed. The proceedings relating to the Basis were apparently never written. There is no doubt, however, that the Basis was adopted on this occasion, it is said, at an adjourned meeting, and in spite of many projects of revision it has with one addition — the phrase about "equal citizenship of women" — remained the Basis of the Society to the present time.

The purpose of the Basis has been often misunderstood. It is not a confession of faith, or a statement of the whole content and meaning of Socialism. It is merely a test of admission, a minimum basis of agreement, acceptance of which is required from those who aspire to share in the control of a Society which had set out to reconstruct our social system. The most memorable part of the discussion was the proposal of Mr. Stuart Glennie to add a clause relating to marriage and the family. This was opposed by Mrs. Besant, then regarded as an extremist on that subject, and was defeated. In view of the large amount of business transacted before the discussion of the Basis began, the debate cannot have been prolonged.

It is easy enough, nearly thirty years later, to criticise this document, to point out that it is purely economic, and unnecessarily rigid: that the phrase about compensation, which has been more discussed than any other, is badly worded, and for practical purposes always disregarded in the constructive proposals of the Society. The best testimony to the merits of the Basis is its survival — its acceptance by the continuous stream of new members who have joined the Society — and it has survived not because its upholders deemed it perfect, but because it has always been found impracticable to put on paper any alternative on which even a few could agree. In fact, proposals to re-write the Basis have on several occasions been referred to Committees, but none of the Committees has ever succeeded in presenting a report.

At the end of the year the sole fruit of the Parliamentary League was published. It is Tract No. 6, entitled "The True Radical Programme" and consists of a declamatory criticism of the official Liberal-Radical Programme announced at Nottingham in October, 1887, and a demand to replace it by the True Radical Programme, namely, adult (in place of manhood) suffrage, payment of Members of Parliament and election expenses, taxation of unearned incomes, nationalisation of railways, the eight hours day, and a few other items. "The above programme," it says, "is sufficient for the present to fill the hands of the True Radical Party — the New Labour Party — in a word, the Practical Socialist Party." It is by no means so able and careful a production as the Report on the Government Organisation of Unemployed Labour.

In April, 1888, the seven Essayists were elected as the Executive Committee, Graham Wallas and William Clarke taking the places of Frank Podmore and W.L. Phillips, who retired, and at the same meeting the Parliamentary League was turned into the Political Committee of the Society; and Tract 7, "Capital and Land," was approved. This tract, the work of Sydney Olivier, is a reasoned attack on Single Tax as a panacea, and in addition contains an estimate of the total realised wealth of the country, just as "Facts for Socialists" does of its income. This, too, has been regularly revised and reprinted ever since and commands a steady sale. It is now in its seventh edition.

Meanwhile the series of meetings, variously described as Public, Ordinary, and Private, was kept on regularly twice a month, with a break only of two months from the middle of July. Most of the meetings were still held in the houses of members, but as early as November, 1886, an ordinary meeting was held at Willis's Rooms, King Street, St. James's, at that time an ultra-respectable rendezvous for societies of the most select character, keeping up an old-fashioned ceremonial of crimson tablecloths, elaborate silver candlesticks, and impressively liveried footmen. Having been turned out of Anderton's Hotel, the Society, on the application of Olivier, was accepted solemnly at Willis's, probably because the managers regarded the mere fact of our venturing to approach them as a certificate of high rank in the world of learned societies.

One meeting of this period is perhaps worthy of record. On 16th March, 1888, Mr. R.B. Haldane, M.P., subsequently Secretary of State for War and Lord Chancellor, addressed the Society on "Radical Remedies for Economic Evils." In the pages of the "Radical," Vol. II, No. 8, for March, 1888, can be found a vivid contemporary account of the proceedings from the pen of Mr. George Standring, entitled "Butchered to Make a Fabian Holiday." After describing the criticism of the lecture by Sidney Webb, Mrs. Besant, and Bernard Shaw the report proceeds:

"The massacre was concluded by two other members of the Society and then the chairman called on Mr. Haldane to reply. Hideous mockery! The chairman knew that Haldane was *dead*! He had seen him torn and tossed and trampled under foot. Perhaps he expected the ghost of the M.P. to rise and conclude the debate with frightful jabberings of fleshless jaws and gestures of bony hands. Indeed I heard a rustling of papers as if one gathered his notes for a speech; but I felt unable to face the grisly horror of a phantom replying to his assassins; so I fled."

It should be added that Mr. Standring did not become a member of the Society until five years later.

By the summer of 1888 the leaders of the Society realised that they had a message for the world, and they decided that the autumn should be devoted to a connected series of lectures on the "Basis and Prospects of Socialism" which should subsequently be published.

There is no evidence, however, that the Essayists supposed that they were about to make an epoch in the history of Socialism. The meetings in the summer had been occupied with lectures by Professor D.G. Ritchie on the "Evolution of Society," subsequently published as his well-known volume "Darwinism and Politics." Walter Crane on "The Prospects of Art under Socialism," Graham Wallas on "The Co-operative Movement," and Miss Clementina Black on "Female Labour." At the last-named meeting, on June 15th, a resolution was moved by H.H. Champion and seconded by Herbert Burrows (neither of them members) calling on the public to boycott Bryant and May's matches on account of the low wages paid. This marks the beginning of the period of Labour Unrest, which culminated in the Dock Strike of the following year.

The first meeting of the autumn was held at Willis's Rooms on September 21st, with the Rev. S.D. Headlam in the chair. The Secretary read a statement indicating the scope of the course of the seven lectures arranged for the Society's meetings during the autumn, after which the first paper, written by Sidney Webb on "The Historical Aspect of the Basis of Socialism," was read by Hubert Bland. Webb had at that time started for a three months' visit to the United States, in which I accompanied him. Mr. Headlam was the chairman throughout the course, except on one occasion, and the lectures continued fortnightly to the 21st December. It does not appear that any special effort was made to advertise them. Each lecture was discussed by members of the Society and of the S.D.F., and with the exception of the Rev. Philip Wicksteed there is no evidence of the presence of any persons outside the movement then or subsequently known to fame.

The preparation of "Fabian Essays" for publication occupied nearly a year, and before dealing with it we must follow the history of the Society during that period.

The first lecture in 1889 was by Edward Carpenter, whose paper, "Civilisation: Its Cause and Cure," gives the title to perhaps his best known volume of essays. Another interesting lecture was by William Morris, entitled "How Shall We Live Then?" and at the Annual Meeting in April Sydney Olivier became the first historian of the Society with an address on "The Origin and Early History of the Fabian Society," for which he made the pencil notes on the minute book already mentioned.

The seven Essayists were re-elected to the Executive, and in the record of proceedings at the meeting there is no mention of the proposed volume of essays.

It is, however, possible to give some account of the organisation and activities for the year ending in March, 1889, since the first printed Annual Report covers that period. It is a four-page quarto document, only a few copies of which are preserved. Of the Society itself but little is recorded — a list of lectures and the bare statement that the autumn series were to be published: the fact that 6500 Fabian Tracts had been distributed and a second edition of 5000 "Facts for Socialists" printed: that 32 members had been elected and 6 had withdrawn — the total is not given — and that the deficit in the Society's funds had been reduced.

A favourite saying of Sidney Webb's is that the activity of the Fabian Society is the sum of the activities of its members. His report as Secretary of the work of the "Lecture Committee" states that a lecture list with 33 names had been printed, and returns made by 31 lecturers recorded 721 lectures during the year. Six courses of lectures on Economics accounted for 52 of these. The "Essays" series of lectures was redelivered by special request in a room lent by King's College, Cambridge, and also at Leicester. Most of the other lectures were given at London Radical Working Men's Clubs, then and for some years later a much bigger factor in politics than they have been in the twentieth century.

But an almost contemporary account of the life of Bernard Shaw, probably the most active of the leaders, because the least fettered by his occupation, is given in Tract 41 under the heading:

"How To Train For Public Life.

"We had to study where we could and how we could. I need not repeat the story of the Hampstead Historic Club, founded by a handful of us to read Marx and Proudhon, and afterwards turned into a systematic history class in which each student took his turn at being professor. My own experience may be taken as typical. For some years I attended the Hampstead Historic Club once a fortnight, and spent a night in the alternate weeks at a private circle of economists which has since blossomed into the British Economic Association—a circle where the social question was left out, and the work kept on abstract scientific lines. I made all my acquaintances think me madder than usual by the pertinacity with which I attended debating societies and haunted all sorts of hole-and-corner debates and public meetings and made speeches at them. I was President of the Local Government Board at an amateur Parliament where a Fabian ministry had to put its proposals into black and white in the shape of Parliamentary Bills. Every Sunday I lectured on some subject which I wanted to teach to myself; and it was not until I had come to the point of being able to deliver separate lectures, without notes, on Rent, Interest, Profits, Wages, Toryism, Liberalism, Socialism, Communism, Anarchism, Trade-Unionism, Co-operation, Democracy, the Division of Society into Classes, and the Suitability of Human Nature to Systems of Just Distribution, that I was able to handle Social-Democracy as it must be handled before it can be preached in such a way as to present it to every sort of man from his own particular point of view. In old lecture lists of the Society you will find my name down for twelve different lectures or so. Nowadays I have only one, for which the secretary is good enough to invent four or five different names. Sometimes I am asked for one of the old ones, to my great dismay, as I forget all about them; but I get out of the difficulty by delivering the new one under the old name, which does as well. I do not hesitate to say that all our best lecturers have two or three old lectures at the back of every single point in their best new speeches; and this means that they have spent a certain number of years plodding away at footling little meetings and dull discussions, doggedly placing these before all private engagements, however tempting. A man's Socialistic acquisitiveness must be keen enough to make him actually prefer spending two or three nights a week in speaking and debating, or in picking up social information even in the most dingy and scrappy way, to going to the theatre, or dancing or drinking, or even sweethearting, if he is to become a really competent propagandist—unless, of course, his daily work is of such a nature as to be in itself a training for political life; and that, we know, is the case with very few of us indeed. It is at such lecturing and debating work, and on squalid little committees and ridiculous little delegations to conferences of the three tailors of Tooley Street, with perhaps a deputation to the Mayor thrown in once in a blue moon or so, that the ordinary Fabian workman or clerk must qualify for his future seat on the Town Council, the School Board, or perhaps in the Cabinet. It was in that way that Bradlaugh, for instance, graduated from being a boy evangelist to being one of the most formidable debaters in the House of Commons. And the only opponents who have ever held their own against the Fabians in debate have been men like Mr. Levy or Mr. Foote, who learnt in the same school."

But lecturing was not the only activity of the Fabians. There were at that time local Groups, each comprising one or a dozen constituencies in London and its suburbs. The Groups in a corporate capacity did little: but the members are reported as taking part in local elections, County Council, School Board, and Vestry, in the meetings of the London Liberal and Radical Union, the National Liberal Federation, the Metropolitan Radical Federation, the Women's Liberal Federation, and so on. This was the year of the first London County Council Election, when the Progressive Party, as it was subsequently named, won an unexpected victory, which proved to be both lasting and momentous for the future of the Metropolis. The only overt part taken by the Fabian Society was its "Questions for Candidates," printed and widely circulated before the election, which gave definiteness and point to the vague ideas of Progressivism then in the air. A large majority of the successful candidates had concurred with this programme. A pamphlet by Sidney Webb, entitled "Wanted a Programme," not published but printed privately, was widely circulated in time for the meeting of the National Liberal Federation at Birmingham, and another by the same author, "The Progress of Socialism," stated to be published by "the Hampstead Society for the Study of Socialism," is reported as in its second edition. This pamphlet was later republished by the Fabian Society as Tract No. 15, "English Progress Towards Social Democracy."

Mrs. Besant and the Rev. Stewart Headlam, standing as Progressives, were elected to the School Board in November, 1888, when Hubert Bland was an unsuccessful candidate.

Finally it may be mentioned that a Universities Committee, with Frank Podmore as Secretary for Oxford and G.W. Johnson for Cambridge, had begun the "permeation" of the Universities, which has always been an important part of the propaganda of the Society.

At the Annual Meeting in April, 1889, the Essayists were re-elected as the Executive Committee and Sydney Olivier as Honorary Secretary, but he only retained the post till the end of the year. I returned to London in October, was promptly invited to resume the work, and took it over in January, 1890.

In July another important tract was approved for publication. "Facts for Londoners," No. 8 in the series, 55 pages of packed statistics sold for 6d., was the largest publication the Society had yet attempted. It is, as its sub-title states: "an exhaustive collection of statistical and other facts relating to the Metropolis, with suggestions for reform on Socialist principles." The latter were in no sense concealed: the Society still waved the red flag in season and out. "The Socialist Programme of immediately practicable reforms for London cannot be wholly dissociated from the corresponding Programme for the kingdom." This is the opening sentence, and it is followed by a page of explanation of the oppression of the workers by the private appropriation of rent and interest, and an outline of the proposed reforms, graduated and differentiated income tax, increased death duties, extension of the Factory Acts, reform of the Poor Law, payment of all public representatives, adult suffrage, and several others.

Then the tract settles down to business. London with its County Council only a few months old was at length waking to self-consciousness: Mr. Charles Booth's "Life and Labour in East London" — subsequently issued as the first part of his monumental work — had just been published; it was the subject of a Fabian lecture by Sidney Webb on May 17th; and interest in the political, economic, and social institutions of the city was general. The statistical facts were at that time practically unknown. They had to be dug out, one by one, from obscure and often unpublished sources, and the work thus done by the Fabian Society led up in later years to the admirable and far more voluminous statistical publications of the London County Council.

The tract deals with area and population; with rating, land values, and housing, with water, trams, and docks, all at that time in the hands of private companies, with gas, markets, City Companies, libraries, public-houses, cemeteries; and with the local government of London, Poor Law Guardians and the poor, the School Board and the schools, the Vestries, District Boards, the County Council, and the City Corporation. It was the raw material of Municipal Socialism, and from this time forth the Society recognised that the municipalisation of monopolies was a genuine part of the Socialist programme, that the transfer from private exploiters to public management at the start, and ultimately by the amortisation of the loans to public ownership, actually was *pro tanto* the transfer from private to public ownership of land and capital, as demanded by Socialists.

Here, in passing, we may remark that there is a legend, current chiefly in the United States, that the wide extension of municipal ownership in Great Britain is due to the advocacy of the Fabian Society. This is very far from the truth. The great provincial municipalities took over the management of their water and gas because they found municipal control alike convenient, beneficial to the citizens, and financially profitable: Birmingham in the seventies was the Mecca of Municipalisation, and in 1882 the Electric Lighting Act passed by Mr. Joseph Chamberlain was so careful of the interests of the public, so strict in the limitations it put upon the possible profits to the investor, that electric lighting was blocked in England for some years, and the Act had to be modified in order that capital might be attracted.

What the Fabian Society did was to point out that Socialism did not necessarily mean the control of all industry by a centralised State; that to introduce Socialism did not necessarily require a revolution because much of it could be brought about piecemeal by the votes of the local electors. And secondly the Society complained that London was singularly backward in municipal management: that the wealthiest city in the world was handed over to the control of exploiters, who made profits from its gas, its water, its docks, and its tramways, whilst elsewhere these monopolies were owned and worked by public authorities who obtained all the advantages for the people of the localities concerned. Moreover, it may be questioned whether the Fabian advocacy of municipalisation hastened or retarded that process in London. In provincial towns municipalisation—the word of course was unknown—had been regarded as of no social or political significance. It was a business matter, a local affair, a question of convenience. In London, partly owing to Fabian advocacy and partly because London had at last a single representative authority with a recognised party system, it became the battle ground of the parties: the claim of the Socialists awakened the Individualists to opposition: and the tramways of London were held as a trench in the world-wide conflict between Socialism and its enemies, whose capture was hailed as an omen of progress by one side, and by the other deplored as the presage of defeat.

"Facts for Londoners" was the work of Sidney Webb, but there is nothing in the tract to indicate this. The publications of the Society were collective works, in that every member was expected to assist in them by criticism and suggestion. Although several of the tracts were lectures or papers written by members for other purposes, and are so described, it was not until the issue in November, 1892, of Tract 42, "Christian Socialism," by the Rev. S.D. Headlam, that the author's name is printed on the title page. The reason for the innovation is obvious: this tract was written by a Churchman for Christians, and whilst the Society as a whole approved the conclusions, the premises commended themselves to but a few. It was therefore necessary that the responsibility of the author should be made clear.

The autumn of 1889 is memorable for the great strike of the London Dockers, which broke out on August 14th, was led by John Burns, and was settled mainly by Cardinal Manning on September 14th. The Fabian Society held no meeting between July 19th and September 20th, and there is nothing in the minutes or the Annual Report to show that the Society as such took any part in the historic conflict. But many of the members as individuals lent their aid to the Dockers in their great struggle, which once for all put an end to the belief that hopeless disorganisation is a necessary characteristic of unskilled labour.

Arising out of the Dock Strike, the special demand of the Socialist section of trade unionists for the next four or five years was a legal eight hours day, and the Fabian Society now for the first time recognised that it could render substantial assistance to the labour movement by putting into a practicable shape any reform which was the current demand of the day.

At the members' meeting on September 20 a committee was appointed to prepare an Eight Hours Bill for introduction into Parliament, and in November this was published as Tract No. 9. It consists of a Bill for Parliament, drawn up in proper form, with explanatory notes. It provided that eight hours should be the maximum working day for Government servants, for railway men, and for miners, and that other trades should be brought in when a Secretary of State was satisfied that a majority of the workers desired it. The tract had a large sale — 20,000 had been printed in six months — and it was specially useful because, in fact, it showed the inherent difficulty of any scheme for universal limitation of the hours of labour.

The Eight Hours Day agitation attained larger proportions than any other working-class agitation in England since the middle of the nineteenth century. For a number of years it was the subject of great annual demonstrations in Hyde Park. It commended itself both to the practical trade unionists, who had always aimed at a reduction in the hours of labour, and to the theoretical socialists, who held that the exploiter's profits came from the final hours of the day's work. The Fabian plan of "Trade Option" was regarded as too moderate, and demands were made for a "Trade Exemption" Bill, that is, a Bill enacting a universal Eight Hours Day, with power to any trade to vote its own exclusion. But the more the subject was discussed, the more obvious the difficulties became, and at last it was recognised that each trade must be dealt with separately. Considerable reductions of hours were meantime effected in particular industries; an eight-hour day became the rule in the Government factories and dockyards; the Board of Trade was empowered to insist on the reduction of unduly long hours of duty on railways; finally in 1908 the Miners' Eight Hours Act became law; and the demand for any general Bill faded away.

The autumn meetings were occupied by a course of lectures at Willis's Rooms on "A Century of Social Movements," by Frank Podmore, William Clarke, Graham Wallas, Hubert Bland, and Mrs. Besant, and with the beginning of the year 1890 we come to the publication of "Fabian Essays," and a new chapter in the History of the Society.

Chapter V "Fabian Essays" and the Lancashire Campaign: 1890-3

"Fabian Essays" published – Astonishing success – A new presentation of Socialism – Reviewed after twenty-five years – Henry Hutchinson – The Lancashire Campaign – Mrs. Besant withdraws – "Fabian News."

Volumes of essays by various writers seldom have any durable place in the history of thought because as a rule they do not present a connected body of ideas, but merely the opinions of a number of people who start from incompatible premises and arrive at inconsistent conclusions. A book, to be effective, must maintain a thesis, or at any rate must be a closely integrated series of propositions, and, as a rule, thinkers strong enough to move the world are too independent to pull together in a team.

"Fabian Essays," the work of seven writers, all of them far above the average in ability, some of them possessing individuality now recognised as exceptional, is a book and not a collection of essays. This resulted from two causes. The writers had for years known each other intimately and shared each other's thoughts; they had hammered out together the policy which they announced; and they had moulded each other's opinions before they began to write. Secondly the book was planned in advance. Its scheme was arranged as a whole, and then the parts were allotted to each author, with an agreement as to the ground to be covered and the method to be adopted, in view of the harmonious whole which the authors had designed. It is not often that circumstances permit of a result so happy. "Fabian Essays" does not cover the whole field of Fabian doctrine, and in later years schemes were often set on foot for a second volume dealing with the application of the principles propounded in the first. But these schemes never even began to be successful. With the passage of time the seven essayists had drifted apart. Each was working at the lines of thought most congenial to himself; they were no longer young and unknown men; some of the seven were no longer available. Anyway, no second series of Essays ever approached completion.

Bernard Shaw was the editor, and those who have worked with him know that he does not take lightly his editorial duties. He corrects his own writings elaborately and repeatedly, and he does as much for everything which comes into his care. The high literary level maintained by the Fabian tracts is largely the result of constant scrutiny and amendment, chiefly by Sidney Webb and Bernard Shaw, although the tract so corrected may be published as the work of some other member.

Although therefore all the authors of "Fabian Essays" were competent, and some of them practised writers, it may be assumed that every phrase was considered, and every word weighed, by the editor before the book went to press.

A circular inviting subscriptions for the book was sent out in the spring, and three hundred copies were subscribed in advance. Arrangements with a publisher fortunately broke down because he declined to have the book printed at a "fair house," and as Mrs. Besant was familiar with publishing—she then controlled, or perhaps *was*, the Freethought Publishing Company, of 63 Fleet Street—the Committee resolved on the bold course of printing and publishing the book themselves. A frontispiece was designed by Walter Crane, a cover by Miss May Morris, and just before Christmas, 1889, the book was issued to subscribers and to the public.

None of us at that time was sufficiently experienced in the business of authorship to appreciate the astonishing success of the venture. In a month the whole edition of 1000 copies was exhausted. With the exception of Mrs. Besant, whose fame was still equivocal, not one of the authors had published any book of importance, held any public office, or was known to the public beyond the circles of London political agitators. The Society they controlled numbered only about 150 members. The subject of their volume was far less understood by the public than is Syndicalism at the present day. And yet a six-shilling book, published at a private dwelling-house and not advertised in the press, or taken round by travellers to the trade, sold almost as rapidly as if the authors had been Cabinet Ministers.

A second edition of 1000 copies was issued in March, 1890: in September Mr. Walter Scott undertook the agency of a new shilling paper edition, 5000 of which were sold before publication and some 20,000 more within a year. In 1908 a sixpenny paper edition with a new preface by the editor was issued by Walter Scott, of which 10,000 were disposed of in a few months, and in all some 46,000 copies of the book have been sold in English editions alone. It is difficult to trace the number of foreign editions and translations. The authors made over to the Society all their rights in the volume, and permission for translation and for publication in the United States has always been freely given. In that country we can trace an edition in 1894, published by Charles E. Brown of Boston, with an Introduction by Edward Bellamy and a Preface of some length on the Fabian Society and its work by William Clarke: and another edition in 1909, published by the Ball Publishing Company of Boston, also with the Introduction on the Fabian Society. A Dutch translation by F.M. Wibaut was published in 1891; in 1806 the Essays, translated into Norwegian by Francis Wolff, appeared as a series of small books; and in 1897 a German translation by Dora Lande was issued by G.H. Wigand of Leipzig.

The effect of "Fabian Essays" arose as much from what it left out as from what it contained. Only the fast-dwindling band of pioneer Socialists, who lived through the movement in its earliest days, can fully realise the environment of ideas from which "Fabian Essays" showed a way of escape.

The Socialism of the Social Democratic Federation and the Socialist League, the two societies which had hitherto represented Socialism to the general public, was altogether revolutionary. Socialism was to be the result of an outbreak of violence, engineered by a great popular organisation like that of the Chartists or the Anti-Corn Law League, and the Commune of Paris in 1871 was regarded as a premature attempt which pointed the way to future success. The Socialist Government thus established was to reconstruct the social and industrial life of the nation according to a plan supposed to be outlined by Karl Marx. "On the morrow of the revolution" all things would be new, and at a bound the nation was expected to reach something very like the millennium.

The case for this project was based, strange to say, not on any history but on the Marxian analysis of the origin of the value of commodities, and no man who did not understand this analysis, or pretend to understand it, was fit to be called a "comrade." The economic reasoning which "proved" this "law" was expressed in obscure and technical language peculiar to the propagandists of the movement, and every page of Socialist writings was studded with the then strange words "proletariat" and "bourgeoisie."

Lastly, the whole world, outside the socialist movement, was regarded as in a conspiracy of repression. Liberals (all capitalists), Tories (all landlords), the Churches (all hypocrites), the rich (all idlers), and the organised workers (all sycophants) were treated as if they fully understood and admitted the claims of the Socialists, and were determined for their own selfish ends to reject them at all costs.

Although the Fabian propaganda had no doubt had some effect, especially amongst the working-class Radicals of London, and although some of the Socialist writers and speakers, such as William Morris, did not at all times present to the public the picture of Socialism just outlined, it will not be denied by anybody whose recollections reach back to this period that Socialism up to 1890 was generally regarded as insurrectionary, dogmatic, Utopian, and almost incomprehensible.

"Fabian Essays" presented the case for Socialism in plain language which everybody could understand. It based Socialism, not on the speculations of a German philosopher, but on the obvious evolution of society as we see it around us. It accepted economic science as taught by the accredited British professors; it built up the edifice of Socialism on the foundations of our existing political and social institutions: it proved that Socialism was but the next step in the development of society, rendered inevitable by the changes which followed from the industrial revolution of the eighteenth century.

It is interesting after twenty-five years to re-read these essays and to observe how far the ideas that inspired them are still valid, and how far the prophecies made have been fulfilled.

Bernard Shaw contributed the first Essay on "The Economic Basis of Socialism," and also a second, a paper read to the British Association in September, 1888, on the "Transition to Social Democracy." His characteristic style retains its charm, although the abstract and purely deductive economic analysis on which he relied no longer commends itself to the modern school of thought. Sidney Webb's "Historic Basis" is as readable as ever, except where he quotes at length political programmes long forgotten, and recounts the achievements of municipal socialism with which we are all now familiar.

William Clarke in explaining the "Industrial Basis" assumed that the industry would be rapidly dominated by trusts — then a new phenomenon — with results, the crushing out of all other forms of industrial organisation, which are but little more evident to-day, though we should no longer think worthy of record that the Standard Oil Company declared a 10 per cent cash dividend in 1887!

If the Essays had been written in 1890 instead of 1888 the authors would have acquired from the great Trade Union upheaval of 1889 a fuller appreciation of the importance of Trade Unionism than they possessed at the earlier date. Working-class organisation has never been so prominent in London as in the industrial counties, and the captious comments on the great Co-operative movement show that the authors of the Essays were still youthful, and in some matters ignorant.

Sydney Olivier's "Moral Basis" is, in parts, as obscure now as it was at first, and there are pages which can have conveyed but little to most of its innumerable readers. Graham Wallas treated of "Property" with moderation rather than knowledge. Time has dealt hardly with Mrs. Besant's contribution. She anticipated, as the other Essayists did, that unemployment caused by labour-saving machinery would constantly increase; and that State organisation of industries for the unemployed would gradually supersede private enterprise. She apparently supposed that the county councils all over England, then newly created, were similar in character to the London County Council, which had already inaugurated the Progressive policy destined in the next few years to do much for the advancement of practical socialism. The final paper on "The Outlook," by Hubert Bland, is necessarily of the nature of prophecy, and in view of the difficulty of this art his attempt is perhaps less unsuccessful than might have been expected. He could foresee the advent neither of the Labour Party, mainly formed of Trade Unionists, nor of Mr. Lloyd George and the policy he represents: he assumed that the rich would grow richer and the poor poorer; that Liberals would unite with Tories, as they have done in Australia, and would be confronted with a Socialist Party representing the dispossessed. Possibly the developments he sketches are still to come, but that is a matter which cannot be discussed here.

I can find no trace in the records of the Society that the first success of their publication occasioned any elation to the Essayists, and I cannot recollect any signs of it at the time. The Annual Report mentions that a substantial profit was realised on the first edition, and states that the authors had made over the copyright, "valued at about £200," to the Society; but these details are included in a paragraph headed "Publications," and the Essays are not mentioned in the general sketch of the work of the year.

In fact the obvious results of the publication took some months to materialise, and the number of candidates for election to the Society showed little increase during the spring. It is true that great changes were made in the organisation of the Society at the Annual Meeting held on March 28th, 1890, but these were in part due to other causes. The Executive Committee was enlarged to fifteen, and as I happened to be available I was appointed paid secretary, half time, at the modest salary of £1 a week for the first year. The newly elected Executive included the seven Essayists, Robert E. Dell, now Paris correspondent for several journals, W.S. De Mattos, for many years afterwards an indefatigable organiser for the Society, and now settled in British Columbia, the Rev. Stewart D. Headlam, Mrs. L.T. Mallet, then a prominent member of the Women's Liberal Association, J.F. Oakeshott, of the Fellowship of the New Life, and myself.

The lectures of the early months of 1890 were a somewhat brilliant series. Sidney Webb on the Eight Hours Bill; James Rowlands, M.P., on the then favourite Liberal nostrum of Leasehold Enfranchisement (which the Essayists demolished in a crushing debate); Dr. Bernard Bosanquet on "The Antithesis between Individualism and Socialism Philosophically Considered"; Mrs. Besant on "Socialism and the School Board Policy"; Mr. (now Sir) H. Llewellyn Smith on "The Causes and Effects of Immigration from Country to Town," in which he disproved the then universal opinion that the unemployed of East London were immigrants from rural districts; Sydney Olivier on "Zola"; William Morris on "Gothic Architecture" (replacing a lecture on Morris himself by Ernest Radford, who was absent through illness); Sergius Stepniak on "Tolstoi, Tchernytchevsky, and the Russian School"; Hubert Bland on "Socialist Novels"; and finally on July 18th Bernard Shaw on "Ibsen." This last may perhaps be regarded as the high-water mark in Fabian lectures. The minutes, which rarely stray beyond bare facts, record that "the paper was a long one," nearer two hours than one, if my memory is accurate, and add: "The meeting was a very large one and the lecture was well received." In fact the lecture was the bulk of the volume "The Quintessence of Ibsenism," which some regard as the finest of Bernard Shaw's works, and it is perhaps unnecessary to say that the effect on the packed audience was overwhelming. It was "briefly discussed" by a number of speakers, but they seemed as out of place as a debate after an oratorio.

On June 16th Henry H. Hutchinson of Derby was elected a member, an event of much greater importance than at the time appeared. Mr. Hutchinson had been clerk to the Justices of Derby, and when we first knew him had retired, and was with his wife living a somewhat wandering life accompanied by a daughter, who also joined the Society a few months later. He was not rich, but he was generous, and on July 29th it is recorded in the minutes of the Executive that he had offered us £100 or £200, and approved the suggestion that it should be chiefly used for lectures in country centres.

A fortnight later the "Lancashire campaign" was planned. It was thoroughly organised. An advanced agent was sent down, and abstracts of lectures were prepared and printed to facilitate accurate reports in the press. Complete lists of the forthcoming lectures — dates, places, subjects, and lecturers — were printed. All the Essayists except Olivier took part, and in addition Robert E. Dell, W.S. De Mattos, and the Rev. Stewart Headlam. An account of the Society written by Bernard Shaw was reprinted from the "Scottish Leader" for September 4th, 1890, for the use of the audience and the Press.

A "Report" of the campaign was issued on November 4th, which says:

> "The campaign began on September 20th and ended on October 27th, when about sixty lectures in all had been delivered ... not only in Lancashire, at Manchester, Liverpool,

Rochdale, Oldham, Preston, Salford, and the district round Manchester, but also at Barnsley, Kendal, Carlisle, Sheffield, and Hebden Bridge.

"In thus making our first attack upon the stronghold of the old Unionism and the new Toryism, we would have been contented with a very small measure of success, and we are much more than contented with the results obtained. The lectures, except for a few days during the contest at Eccles, were extremely well reported, and even the *Manchester Guardia'* (the *Daily News* of the manufacturing districts) came out with an approving leader. The audiences throughout the campaign steadily increased and followed the lectures with close and intelligent attention. In particular the members of Liberal working men's clubs constantly declared that they had never heard 'the thing put so straight' before, and complained that the ordinary party lecturers were afraid or unwilling to speak out. Men who frankly confessed that they had hesitated before voting for the admission of our lecturers to their clubs were enthusiastic in welcoming our message as soon as they heard it. The vigorous propaganda in the manufacturing districts of the S.D.F. branches has been chiefly carried on by means of outdoor meetings. Its effect upon working-class opinion, especially among unskilled labourers, has been marked and important, but it has entirely failed to reach the working-men politicians who form the rank and file of the Liberal Associations and Clubs, or the 'well-dressed' Liberals who vaguely desire social reform, but have been encouraged by their leaders to avoid all exact thought on the subject."

The lectures were given chiefly in sets of four in consecutive weeks, mostly at Liberal and Radical Clubs: others were arranged by Co-operative Societies, and by branches of the S.D.F. and the Socialist League. The subjects were "Socialism," "Where Liberalism Fails," "Co-operation and Labour," "The Future of Women," "The Eight Hours Bill," "The Politics of Labour," and so on. Those arranged by Co-operative Societies were, we are told, the least successful, but it is hoped "that they will bring about a better feeling between Socialists and Co-operators," a state of things which on the side of the Socialists was, as we have previously indicated, badly wanted. It should be noted that much of the success of the campaign was due to friendly assistance from the head-quarters of the Co-operative Union and the National Reform Union.

There is no doubt that this campaign with the series of lectures on the same lines which were continued for several years was an event of some importance, not only in the history of the Fabian Society but also in English politics. Hitherto the Socialism presented to the industrial districts of England, which are the backbone of Trade Unionism and Co-operation, to the men who are meant when we speak of the power and independence of the working classes, was revolutionary and destructive, ill-tempered and ungenerous. It had perhaps alarmed, but it had failed to attract them. It had made no real impression on the opinion of the people. From this point a new movement began. It first took the form of local Fabian Societies. They were succeeded by and merged into branches of the Independent Labour Party, which adopted everything Fabian except its peculiar political tactics. A few years later the Labour Party followed, more than Fabian in its toleration in the matter of opinions, and virtually, though not formally, Fabian in its political policy. No doubt something of the sort would have happened had there never been a Lancashire campaign, but this campaign may be fairly described as the first step in an evolution, the end of which is not yet in sight.

Her lectures in the Lancashire campaign and the formation of the branches were Mrs. Besant's last contributions to the Socialist movement. Early in November she suddenly and completely severed her connection with the Society. She had become a convert to Theosophy, which at that time accepted the Buddhist doctrine that spiritual conditions alone mattered, and that spiritual life would flourish as well in the slum amidst dirt and starvation as in the comfortable cottage, and much better than in the luxurious mansion. Twentieth-century theosophy has receded from that position, and now advocates social amelioration, but Mrs. Besant thought otherwise in 1890. Some twenty years later she lectured on several occasions to the Society, and she joined her old friends at the dinner which celebrated the thirtieth anniversary of its foundation, but in the interval her connection with it completely ceased.

The Fabian Society and British Socialism owe much to Mrs. Besant for the assistance she gave it during five important years. Her splendid eloquence, always at our service, has seldom been matched, and has never been surpassed by any of the innumerable speakers of the movement. She had, when she joined us, an assured position amongst the working-class Radicals in London and throughout the country; and through her Socialism obtained a sympathetic hearing in places where less trusted speakers would have been neglected. She was not then either a political thinker or an effective worker on committees, but she possessed the power of expressing the ideas of other people far better than their originators, and she had at her command a certain amount of political machinery — such as an office at 63 Fleet Street, and a monthly magazine, "Our Corner" — which was very useful. Her departure was a serious loss, but it came at a moment of rapid expansion, so rapid that her absence was scarcely felt.

On the Society itself the effect of the Essays and the Lancashire Campaign was considerable. As the Executive Committee report in April, 1891: "During the past year the Socialist movement has made conspicuous progress in every respect, and a constantly increasing share of the work of its organisation and extension has fallen to the Fabian Society." The membership increased from 173 to 361, and the subscription list — thanks in part to several large donations — from £126 to £520. Local Fabian Societies had been formed at Belfast, Birmingham, Bombay, Bristol, Huddersfield, Hyde, Leeds, Manchester, Oldham, Plymouth, Tyneside, and Wolverhampton, with a total membership of 350 or 400. The business in tracts had been enormous. Ten new tracts, four pamphlets and six leaflets, were published, and new editions of all but one of the old ones had been printed. In all 335,000 tracts were printed and 98,349 distributed. The new tracts include "The Workers' Political Programme," "The New Reform Bill," "English Progress Towards Social Democracy," "The Reform of Poor Law," and a leaflet, No. 13, "What Socialism Is," which has been in circulation ever since. It should be added that at this period our leaflets were given away freely, a form of propaganda which soon proved too expensive for our resources.

In March, 1891, just before the end of the official year, appeared the first number of "Fabian News," the monthly organ of the Society, which has continued ever since. It replaced the printed circulars previously issued to the members, and was not intended to be anything else than a means of communicating with the members as to the work of the Society, and also in later years as to new books on subjects germane to its work. It has been edited throughout by the Secretary, but everything of a contentious character relating to the affairs of the Society has been published by the express authority of the Executive Committee.

It may be mentioned that from this time forward the documents of the Society are both fuller and more accessible than before. For the period up to the end of 1889 the only complete record is contained in the two minute books of the meetings. No regular minutes of Executive Committee meetings were kept, and the Annual Reports were not printed until 1889. From 1890 onwards the meetings of every committee were regularly recorded: the Annual Reports were printed in octavo and can be found in many public libraries, whilst "Fabian News" contains full information of the current doings of the Society. It will not therefore be necessary to treat the later years with such attention to detail as has seemed appropriate to the earlier. The only "sources" for these are shabby notebooks and the memories of a few men now rapidly approaching old age. The later years can be investigated, if any subsequent enquirer desires to do so, in a dozen libraries in Great Britain and the United States.

Chapter VI   "To your tents, O Israel": 1894-1900

Progress of the Society – The Independent Labour Party – Local Fabian Societies – University Fabian Societies – London Groups and Samuel Butler – The first Fabian Conference – Tracts and Lectures – The 1892 Election Manifesto – The Newcastle Program – The Fair Wages Policy – The "Fortnightly" article – The "Intercepted Letter" of 1906.

During the next two or three years the Society made rapid progress. The membership was 541 in 1892, 640 in 1893, and 681 in 1894. The expenditure, £640 to March, 1891, rose to £1100 for 1892, and £1179 in 1893. In both these years large sums — £350 and £450 — were given by two members for the expenses of lectures in the provinces, and in provincial societies the growth was most marked. In March, 1892, 36 were recorded: the report for 1893 gives 74, including Bombay and South Australia. This was the high-water mark. The Independent Labour Party was founded in January, 1893, at a Conference at which the Fabian Society of London and nine local Fabian Societies were represented, and from this time onward our provincial organisation declined until, in 1900, only four local and four University Societies remained.

The attitude of the parent society towards its branches has always been somewhat unusual. In early days it made admission to its own ranks a matter of some difficulty. A candidate resident in London had to secure a proposer and seconder who could personally vouch for him and had to attend two meetings as a visitor. We regarded membership as something of a privilege, and a candidate was required not only to sign the Basis, but also to take some personal trouble as evidence of zeal and good faith. To our provincial organisation the same principle was applied. If the Socialists in any town desired to form a local society we gave them our blessing and received them gladly. But we did not urge the formation of branches on lukewarm adherents, and we always recognised that the peculiar political methods of the London Society, appropriate to a body of highly educated people, nearly all of them speakers, writers, or active political workers, were unsuitable for the groups of earnest workmen in the provinces who were influenced by our teaching. In fact the local Fabian Societies, with rare exceptions, of which Liverpool was the chief, were from the first "I.L.P." in personnel and policy, and were Fabian only in name.

This somewhat detached attitude, combined with the recognition of the differences between the parent society and its offspring, led to the adoption of a system of local autonomy. The parent society retained complete control over its own affairs. It was governed by a mass meeting of members, which in those days elected the Executive for the year. It decided that a local Fabian Society might be formed anywhere outside London, by any body of people who accepted the Fabian Basis. The parent society would send them lecturers, supply them with literature and "Fabian News," and report their doings in the "News." But in other respects complete autonomy was accorded. No fees were asked, or subventions granted: no control over, or responsibility for, policy was claimed. Just as the political policy of each Fabian was left to his own judgment, so we declined the impossible task of supervising or harmonising the political activities of our local societies. When the I.L.P. was founded in Bradford and set to work to organise Socialism on Fabian lines, adopting practically everything of our policy, except the particular methods which we had selected because they suited our personal capacities, we recognised that provincial Fabianism had done its work. There was no room, except here and there, for an I.L.P. branch and a local F.S. in the same place. The men who were active in the one were active also in the other. We made no effort to maintain our organisation against that of the I.L.P., and though a few societies survived for some years, and for a while two or three were formed every year at such places as

Tunbridge Wells, Maidstone, and Swindon, they were bodies of small importance, and contributed scarcely anything to the sum of Fabian activity. The only local Fabian Society which survived the debacle was Liverpool, which has carried on work similar to that of the London Society down to the present time. Its relations with the I.L.P. have always been harmonious, and, like the I.L.P., it has always maintained an attitude of hostility towards the old political parties. Its work has been lecturing, the publication of tracts, and political organisation.

The University Fabian Societies are of a different character. Formed by and for undergraduates, but in some cases, especially at Oxford, maintaining continuity by the assistance of older members in permanent residence, such as Sidney Ball of St. John's, who has belonged to the Oxford Society since its formation in 1895, they are necessarily fluctuating bodies, dependent for their success on the personality and influence of a few leading members. Their members have always been elected at once to the parent society in order that the connection may be unbroken when they leave the University. Needless to say, only a small proportion become active members of the Society, but a few of the leading members of the movement have entered it in this way. Oxford, Glasgow, Aberystwyth, and latterly Cambridge have had flourishing societies for long periods, and quite a number of the higher grade civil servants and of the clergy and doctors in remote districts in Wales and Scotland are or have been members. Moreover, the Society always retains a scattering of members, mostly officials or teachers, in India, in the heart of Africa, in China, and South America, who joined it in their undergraduate days.

Almost from the first the Executive has endeavoured to organise the members in the London area into groups. The parent society grew up through years of drawing-room meetings; why should not the members residing in Hampstead and Hammersmith, in Bloomsbury or Kensington do the same? Further, the Society always laid much stress on local politics: there were County Council and Borough Council, School Board and Poor Law Guardians elections in which policy could be influenced and candidates promoted or supported.

In fact it is only in the years when London government was in the melting-pot, or in times of special socialist activity, and in a few districts, such as Hampstead, where Fabians are numerous, and especially when one or more persons of persistence and energy are available, that the groups have had a more than nominal existence.

The drawing-room meetings of the parent society attracted audiences until they outgrew drawing-rooms, because of the exceptional quality of the men and women who attended them and the novelty of the doctrines promulgated. These conditions were not repeated in each district of London, and in spite of constant paper planning, and not a little service by the older members, who spent their time and talents on tiny meetings in Paddington or Streatham, the London group system has never been a permanent success. What has kept the Society together is the series of fortnightly meetings carried on regularly from the first, which themselves fluctuate in popularity, but which have never wholly failed.

We now return to the point whence this digression started. Our local societies were then flourishing. They were vigorously supported from London. We had funds for the expenses of lecturers and many willing to give the time. W.S. De Mattos was employed as lecture secretary, and arranged in the year 1891-2 600 lectures, 300 of them in the provinces. In all 3339 lectures by members during the year were recorded. All this activity imparted for a time considerable vitality to the local societies, and on February 6th and 7th, 1892, the first (and for twenty years the last) Annual Conference was held in London, at Essex Hall. Only fourteen provincial societies were represented, but they claimed a membership of about 1100, some four-fifths of the whole.

The Conference was chiefly memorable because it occasioned the preparation of the paper by Bernard Shaw, entitled "The Fabian Society: What it has done and how it has done it," published later as Tract 41 and renamed, when the passage of years rendered the title obsolete, "The Fabian Society: Its Early History," parts of which have already been quoted. This entertaining account of the Society, and brilliant defence of its policy as opposed to that of the Social Democratic Federation, was read to a large audience on the Saturday evening, and made so great an impression that comment on it seemed futile and was abandoned. The Conference on Sunday was chiefly occupied with the discussion of a proposal that the electors be advised to vote at the coming General Election in accordance with certain test questions, which was defeated by 23 to 21. A resolution to expel from the Society any member becoming "an official of the

Conservative, Liberal, Liberal Unionist, or National League parties" was rejected by a large majority, for the first but by no means for the last time. The Conference was quite a success, but a year later there was not sufficient eagerness in the provinces for a second, and the project was abandoned.

Amidst all this propaganda of the principles of Socialism the activity of the Society in local government was in no way relaxed. The output of tracts at this period was remarkable. In the year 1890-1, 10 new tracts were published, 335,000 copies printed, and 98,349 sold or given away. In 1891-2, 20 tracts, 16 of them leaflets of 4 pages, were published, 308,300 printed, and 378,281 distributed, most of them leaflets. This was the maximum. Next year only 272,660 were distributed, though the sales of penny tracts were larger. At this period the Society had a virtual monopoly in the production of political pamphlets in which facts and figures were marshalled in support of propositions of reform in the direction of Socialism. Immense trouble was taken to ensure accuracy and literary excellence. Many of the tracts were prepared by Committees which held numerous meetings. Each of them was criticised in proof both by the Executive and by all the members of the Society. Every tract before publication had to be approved at a meeting of members, when the author or authors had to consider every criticism and justify, amend, or delete the passage challenged.

The tracts published in these years included a series of "Questions" for candidates for Parliament and all the local governing bodies embodying progressive programmes of administration with possible reforms in the law — which the candidate was requested to answer by a local elector and which were used with much effect for some years — and a number of leaflets on Municipal Socialism, extracted from "Facts for Londoners." In 1891 the first edition of "What to Read: A List of Books for Social Reformers," classified in a somewhat elaborate fashion, was prepared by Graham Wallas, the fifth edition of which, issued as a separate volume in 1910, is still in print. "Facts for Bristol," drafted by the gentleman who is now Sir Hartmann Just, K.C.M.G., C.B., was the only successful attempt out of many to apply the method of "Facts for Londoners" to other cities.

It is impossible for me to estimate how far the Progressive policy of London in the early nineties is to be attributed to the influence of the Fabian Society. That must be left to the judgment of those who can form an impartial opinion. Something, however, the Society must have contributed to create what was really a remarkable political phenomenon. London up to 1906 was Conservative in politics by an overwhelming majority. In 1892 out of 59 seats the Liberals secured 23, but in 1895 and 1900 they obtained no more than 8 at each election. All this time the Progressive Party in the County Council, which came into office unexpectedly after the confused election in 1889 when the Council was created, maintained itself in power usually by overwhelming majorities, obtained at each succeeding triennial elections in the same constituencies and with substantially the same electorate that returned Conservatives to Parliament.

In the early nineties the Liberal and Radical Working Men's Clubs of London had a political importance which has since entirely disappeared. Every Sunday for eight months in the year, and often on weekdays, political lectures were arranged, which were constantly given by Fabians. For instance, in October, 1891, I find recorded in advance twelve courses of two to five lectures each, nine of them at Clubs, and fifteen separate lectures at Clubs, all given by members of the Society. In October, 1892, eleven courses and a dozen separate lectures by our members at Clubs are notified. These were all, or nearly all, arranged by the Fabian office, and it is needless to say that a number of others were not so arranged or were not booked four or five weeks in advance. Our list of over a hundred lecturers, with their subjects and private addresses, was circulated in all directions and was constantly used by the Clubs, as well as by all sorts of other societies which required speakers.

Moreover, in addition to "Facts for Londoners," Sidney Webb published in 1891 in Sonnenschein's "Social Science Series" a volume entitled "The London Programme," which set out his policy, and that of the Society, on all the affairs of the metropolis. The Society had at this time much influence through the press. "The London Programme" had appeared as a series of articles in the Liberal weekly "The Speaker." The "Star," founded in 1888, was promptly "collared," according to Bernard Shaw, who was its musical critic, and who wrote in it, so it was said, on every subject under the sun except music! Mr. H.W. Massingham, assistant editor of the "Star," was elected to the Society and its Executive simultaneously in March,

1891, and in 1892 he became assistant editor of the "Daily Chronicle," under a sympathetic chief, Mr. A.E. Fletcher.

Mrs. Besant and the Rev. Stewart Headlam had been elected to the London School Board in 1888, and had there assisted a Trade Union representative in getting adopted the first Fair Wages Clause in Contracts. But in the first London County Council the Society, then a tiny body, was not represented.

At the second election in 1892 six of its members were elected to the Council and another was appointed an alderman. Six of these were members best known to the public as Trade Unionists or in other organisations, but Sidney Webb, who headed the poll at Deptford with 4088 votes, whilst his Progressive colleague received 2503, and four other candidates only 5583 votes between them, was a Fabian and nothing else. He had necessarily to resign his appointment in the Colonial Office, and thenceforth was able to devote all his time to politics and literary work. Webb was at once elected chairman of the Technical Education Board, which up to 1904 had the management of all the education in the county, other than elementary, which came under public control. The saying is attributed to him that according to the Act of Parliament Technical Education could be defined as any education above elementary except Greek and Theology, and the Board under his chairmanship—he was chairman for eight years—did much to bring secondary and university education within the reach of the working people of London. From 1892 onwards there was always a group of Fabians on the London County Council, working in close alliance with the "Labour Bench," the Trade Unionists who then formed a group of the Progressive Party under the leadership of John Burns. Under this silent but effective influence the policy of the Progressives was largely identical with the immediate municipal policy of the Society itself, and the members of the Society took a keen and continuous interest in the triennial elections and the work of the Council.

All this concern in local administration did not interfere with the interest taken by the Society in parliamentary politics, and one illustration of this may be mentioned. The Liberal Party has a traditional feud with Landlordism, and at this period its favourite panacea was Leasehold Enfranchisement, that is, the enactment of a law empowering leaseholders of houses built on land let for ninety-nine years, the common practice in London, to purchase the freehold at a valuation. Many Conservatives had come round to the view that the breaking up of large town estates and the creation of numerous freeholders, would strengthen the forces upholding the rights of property, and there was every prospect that the Bill would be passed. A few hours before the debate on April 29th, 1891, a leaflet (Tract No. 22) was published explaining the futility of the proposal from the Fabian standpoint, and a copy was sent to every member of Parliament. To the astonishment of the Liberal leaders a group of Radicals, including the present Lord Haldane and Sir Edward Grey, opposed the Bill, and it was defeated by the narrow majority of 13 in a house numbering 354. A few years later the proposal was dropped out of the Liberal programme, and the Leasehold Enfranchisement Association itself adopted a new name and a revised policy.

But the main object of the Fabians was to force on the Liberal Party a programme of constructive social reform. With few exceptions their members belonged or had belonged to that party, and it was not difficult, now that London had learned the value of the Progressive policy, to get resolutions accepted by Liberal Associations demanding the adoption of a programme. Sidney Webb in 1888 printed privately a paper entitled "Wanted a Programme: An Appeal to the Liberal Party," and sent it out widely amongst the Liberal leaders. The "Star" and the "Daily Chronicle" took care to publish these resolutions, and everything was done, which skilful agitators knew, to make a popular demand for a social reform programme. We did what all active politicians in a democratic country must do; we decided what the people ought to want, and endeavoured to do two things, which after all are much the same thing, to make the people want it, and to make it appear that they wanted it. The result—how largely attributable to our efforts can hardly now be estimated—was the Newcastle Program, reluctantly blessed by Mr. Gladstone and adopted by the National Liberal Federation in 1891.

The General Election of 1892 was anticipated with vivid interest. Since the election of 1886 English Socialism had come into being and Trade Unionism had been transformed by the rise of the Dockers, and the other "new" unions of unskilled labour. But a Labour Party was still in the future, and our Election Manifesto (Tract 40), issued in June, bluntly tells the working classes that until they form a party of their own they will have to choose between the parties belonging to the other classes. The Manifesto, written by Bernard Shaw, is a brilliant essay on labour in politics and a criticism of both the existing parties; it assures the working classes that they could create their own party if they cared as much about politics as they cared for horse-racing (football was not in those days the typical sport); and it concludes by advising them to vote for the better, or against the worse, man, on the ground that progress was made by steps, a step forward was better than a step backward, and the only thing certain is the defeat of a party which sulks and does not vote at all. The Manifesto was widely circulated by the then vigorous local societies, and no doubt had some effect, though the intensity of the antipathy to Liberal Unionism on the one side and to Home Rule on the other left little chance for other considerations.

Six members of the Society were candidates, but none of them belonged to the group which had made its policy and conducted its campaign. In one case, Ben Tillett at West Bradford, the Society took an active part in the election, sending speakers and collecting £152 for the Returning Officer's expenses. Of the six, J. Keir Hardie at West Ham alone was successful, but Tillett did well at West Bradford, polling 2,749, only a few hundred votes below the other two candidates, and preparing the field for the harvest which F.W. Jowett reaped in 1906.

The result of the election, which took place in July, was regarded as a justification for the Fabian policy of social advance. In London, where Liberalism was strongly tainted with it, the result was "as in 1885," the year of Liberal victory, and the only Liberal seat lost was that of the President of the Leasehold Enfranchisement Association! In the industrial cities, and in Scotland, where Liberalism was still individualist, the result was rather as in 1886, when Liberalism lost. In London also "by far the largest majorities were secured by Mr. John Burns and Mr. Keir Hardie, who stood as avowed Socialists, and by Mr. Sydney Buxton, whose views are really scarcely less advanced than theirs."

I have pointed out that Fabian policy began with State Socialism, and in quite early days added to it Municipal Socialism; but in 1888 the authors of "Fabian Essays" appeared to be unconscious of Trade Unionism and hostile to the Co-operative movement. The Dock Strike of 1889 and the lecturing in London clubs and to the artisans of the north pointed the way to a new development. Moreover, in the summer of 1892 Sidney Webb had married Miss Beatrice Potter, author of an epoch-making little book, "The Co-operative Movement," and together they were at work on their famous "History of Trade Unionism."

The "Questions" for local governing bodies issued in 1892 were full of such matters as fair wages, shorter hours, and proper conditions for labour, and it was speedily discovered that this line of advance was the best suited to Fabian tactics because it was a series of skirmishes all over the country, in which scores and hundreds could take part. Each locality had then or soon afterwards three or four elected local councils, and hardly any Fabian from one end of the country to the other would be unable in one way or another to strike a blow or lift a finger for the improvement of the conditions of publicly employed labour.

But the Government of Mr. Gladstone had not been in office for much more than a year before a much more ambitious enterprise on this line was undertaken. In March, 1893, Sir Henry (then Mr.) Campbell-Bannerman had pledged the Government to "show themselves to be the best employers of labour in the country": "we have ceased," he said, "to believe in what are known as competition or starvation wages." That was a satisfactory promise, but enunciating a principle is one thing and carrying it into effect in scores of departments is another. Mr. Gladstone, of course, was interested only in Home Rule. Permanent officials doubtless obstructed, as they usually do: and but a few members of the Cabinet accepted or understood the new obligation. The Fabian Society knew the Government departments from the inside, and it was easy for the Executive to ascertain how labour was treated under each chief, what he had done and what he had left undone. At that time legislative reforms were difficult because the Government majority was both small and uncertain, whilst the whole time of Parliament was occupied by the necessary but futile struggle to pass a Home Rule Bill for the Lords to destroy. But administrative reforms were subject to no such limitations: wages and conditions of labour were determined by the department concerned, and each minister could do what he chose for the workmen virtually in his employment, except perhaps in the few cases, such as the Post Office, where the sums involved were very large, when the Chancellor of the Exchequer had the same opportunity.

Bernard Shaw and Sidney Webb then decided that the time had come to make an attack on old-fashioned Liberalism on these lines.

The "Fortnightly Review" accepted their paper, the Society gave the necessary sanction, and in November the article entitled "To Your Tents, O Israel" appeared. Each of the great departments of the State was examined in detail, and for each was stated precisely what should be done to carry out the promise that the Government would be "in the first flight of employers," and what in fact had been done, which indeed, with rare exceptions, was nothing. The "Parish Councils Act" and Sir William Harcourt's great Budget of 1894 were still in the future, and so far there was little to show as results from the Liberal victory of the previous year. The case against the Government from the Labour standpoint was therefore unrelieved black, and the Society, in whose name the Manifesto appeared, called on the working classes to abandon Liberalism, to form a Trade Union party of their own, to raise £30,000 and to finance fifty candidates for Parliament. It is a curious coincidence that thirteen years later, in 1906, the Party formed, as the Manifesto demanded, by the big Trade Unions actually financed precisely fifty candidates and succeeded in electing thirty of them.

The Manifesto led to the resignation of a few distinguished members, including Professor D.G. Ritchie, Mrs. Bateson, widow of the Master of St. John's College, Cambridge, and more important than all the rest, Mr. H.W. Massingham. He was on the Continent when the Manifesto was in preparation; otherwise perhaps he might have come to accept it: for his reply, which was published in the same magazine a month later, was little more than a restatement of the case. "The only sound interpretation of a model employer," he said, "is a man who pays trade union rates of wages, observes trade union limit of hours, and deals with 'fair' as opposed to 'unfair' houses. Apply all these tests and the Government unquestionably breaks down on every one of them." If this was all that an apologist for the Government could say, no wonder that the attack went home. The opponents of Home Rule were of course delighted to find another weak spot in their adversary's defences; and the episode was not soon forgotten.

In January the article was reprinted with much additional matter drafted by Bernard Shaw. He showed in considerable detail how a Labour Party ought to be formed, and how, in fact, it was formed seven years later. With our numerous and still flourishing local societies, and the newly formed I.L.P., a large circulation for the tract was easily secured. Thousands of working-class politicians read and remembered it, and it cannot be doubted that the "Plan of Campaign for Labour," as it was called, did much to prepare the ground for the Labour Party which was founded so easily and flourished so vigorously in the first years of the twentieth century.

At this point the policy of simple permeation of the Liberal Party may be said to have come to an end. The "Daily Chronicle," under the influence of Mr. Massingham, became bitterly hostile to the Fabians. They could no longer plausibly pretend that they looked for the realisation of their immediate aims through Liberalism. They still permeated, of course, since they made no attempt to form a party of their own, and they believed that only through existing organisations, Trade Unions on one side, the political parties on the other, could sufficient force be obtained to make progress within a reasonable time. In one respect it must be confessed we shared an almost universal delusion. When the Liberal Party was crushed at the election of 1895 we thought that its end had come in England as it has in other countries. Conservatism is intelligible: Socialism we regarded as entirely reasonable. Between the two there seemed to be no logical resting place. We had discovered long ago that the working classes were not going to rush into Socialism, but they appeared to be and were in fact growing up to it. The Liberalism of the decade 1895-1905 had measures in its programme, such as Irish Home Rule, but it had no policy, and it seemed incredible then, as it seems astonishing now, that a party with so little to offer could sweep the country, as it was swept by the Liberals in 1906. But nobody could have foreseen Mr. Lloyd George, and although the victory of 1906 was not due to his leadership, no one can doubt that it is his vigorous initiative in the direction of Socialism which secured for his party the renewed confidence of the country.

Twelve years later another attempt to get administrative reform from the Liberal Party was made on somewhat similar lines. The party had taken office in December, 1905, and in the interval before the General Election of 1906 gave them their unprecedented majority, "An Intercepted Letter," adopted at a members' meeting in December, was published in the "National Review" for January. It purported to be a circular letter addressed by the Prime Minister to his newly appointed colleagues, giving each of them in turn advice how to run his department. In this case there was no necessity to suggest administrative reforms only. The Liberals were certain of a majority, and they had no programme: they were bound to win, not on their merits, but on the defects of their opponents. The Letter, written by Webb in a rollicking style, to which he rarely condescends, touched on each of the great departments of Government, and advocated both the old policy of Trade Union hours and wages, for which the new Prime Minister had made himself in 1893 personally responsible, but also all sorts of progressive measures, graduated and differentiated income-tax for the Treasury, Compulsory Arbitration in Labour Disputes for the Home Office — we discovered the flaw in that project later — reform of Grants in Aid for the Local Government Board, Wages Boards for Agriculture, and so on. A few weeks later the country had the General Election to think about, and the Letter was merely reprinted for private circulation amongst the members of the Society. But we took care that the new Ministers read it, and it served to remind them of the demands which, after the election, the Labour Party, at last in being, would not let them again forget.

Chapter VII "Fabianism and the Empire": 1900-1

The Library and Book Boxes — Parish Councils — The Workmen's Compensation Act — The Hutchinson Trust — The London School of Economics — Educational Lectures — Electoral Policy — The controversy over the South African War — The publication of "Fabianism and the Empire."

The next few years were devoted to quieter work than that of the period described in the previous chapter. The Conservative Party was in power, Liberalism, which had lost its great leader, and a year or two later lost also his successor, Lord Rosebery, was in so hopeless a minority that its return to power in the near future seemed to be and was impossible. It had been easy to permeate the Liberals, because most of our members were or had been connected with their party. It was impossible to permeate Conservatism on similar lines, both because we were not in touch with their organisation and because Conservatives in general regarded our proposals with complete aversion. It was a time, therefore, for educational rather than political activity, and to this the Society devoted the greater part of its energies. Its work in this field took various forms, some of which may be briefly described.

We had started a lending library in boxes for our local societies, and as these died away we offered the use of it to working-class organisations, and indeed to any organisation of readers or students. Books were purchased from special funds, a collection of some 5000 volumes was ultimately formed, and for the last twenty years the Society has kept in circulation anything up to 200 boxes of books on Socialism, economics, history and social problems, which are lent for ten shillings a year to Co-operative Societies, Trade Unions, Socialist Societies, and miscellaneous organisations. The books are intended to be educational rather than directly propagandist, and each box is made up to suit the taste, expressed or inferred, of the subscriber. Quarterly exchanges are allowed, but the twenty or thirty books in a box usually last a society for a year. It is a remarkable fact that although boxes are lent freely to such slight organisations as reading classes, and are sent even to remote mining villages in Wales or Scotland, not a single box has ever been lost. Delays are frequent: books of course are often missing, but sooner or later every box sent out has been returned to the Society.

Another method of securing the circulation of good books on social subjects has been frequently used. We prepare a list of recent and important publications treating of social problems and request each member to report how many of them are in the Public Library of his district, and further to apply for the purchase of such as are absent.

The Local Government Act of 1894, commonly called the Parish Councils Act, which constituted out of chaos a system of local government for rural England, gave the Society an opportunity for practising that part of its policy which includes the making the best use of all forms of existing legislation. Mr. Herbert Samuel was at that time a friend, though he was never a member, of the Society, and the first step in his successful political career was his candidature for the typically rural Southern Division of Oxfordshire. He was good enough to prepare for us not only an admirable explanation of the Act, but also Questions for Parish Councillors, for Rural District Councillors, and for Urban District Councillors. Probably this was the first time that an analysis of a new Act of Parliament had been published at a penny. Anyway the demand for it was considerable, and over 30,000 copies were sold in five months. Then it was revised, with the omission of temporary matter, and republished as "Parish and District Councils: What they are and what they can do," and in this form has gone through many editions, and is still in print. The tract states that the secretary of the Society will give advice on any obscure point in the law, and in this way the Society has become an Information Bureau; hardly a week passed for many years after the autumn of 1895 without a letter from some village or small town asking questions as to housing, common rights, charities, the duties of chairmen of councils, the qualifications of candidates, and so on.

Similar tracts were published describing the powers and duties of the London County Council, the London Vestries, and the Metropolitan Borough Councils, established in 1899, while one giving the powers of various local authorities for housing (No. 76, "Houses for the People") has gone through many editions and still has a steady sale.

The Workmen's Compensation Act, 1897, afforded another opportunity for this sort of work. Our penny tract (No. 82) describing the rights of the workmen under the Act was reprinted thirteen times in eight months, and over 120,000 were sold in the first year of publication. This tract offered free advice to every purchaser, and the result has been an enormous amount of correspondence which during seventeen years has never entirely ceased. This work of providing expert advice on minor legal matters has been a quiet service to the community constantly rendered by the Society. The barristers amongst our members have freely given assistance in the more difficult matters. Occasionally the solicitors amongst us have taken up cases where the plaintiff was specially helpless.

In 1894, Henry Hutchinson, who had provided the funds for much of our country lecturing, died, and to our complete surprise it was found that he had appointed Sidney Webb, whom he hardly knew personally, his executor, and had left the residue of his estate, between £9000 and £10,000, to five trustees—Sidney Webb, his daughter, myself, William Clarke, and W.S. De Mattos—with directions that the whole sum be expended within ten years. The two last named took but little part in administering the trust, and Miss Hutchinson died only fifteen months later, also leaving to her colleagues the residue of her estate, something under £1000, for similar purposes. The trustees—Mrs. Bernard Shaw, Hubert Bland, and Frederick Whelen were appointed at later dates—resolved that the money in their charge should be used exclusively for special work, as otherwise the effect would be merely to relieve the members of their obligation to pay for the maintenance of their Society. They decided to devote part of the funds to initiating the London School of Economics and Political Science, because they considered that a thorough knowledge of these sciences was a necessity for people concerned in social reconstruction, if that reconstruction was to be carried out with prudence and wisdom: and in particular it was essential that all classes of public officials should have the opportunity of learning whatever can be known of economics and politics taught on modern lines. Our old Universities provided lectures on political science as it was understood by Plato and Aristotle, by Hobbes and Bentham: they did not then—and indeed they do not now—teach how New Zealand deals with strikes, how America legislates about trusts, how municipalities all over the world organise tramways.

The trustees, as I have said, originated the London School of Economics, but from the first they associated others with themselves in its management, and they made no attempt to retain any special share in its control. Their object was to get taught the best science that could be obtained, confident that if their own political theories were right, science would confirm them, and if they were wrong, it was better that they should be discredited. The London School of Economics, though thus founded, has never had any direct or organic connection with the Fabian Society, and therefore any further account of its successful career would be out of place in this volume. But it may be said that it has certainly more than justified the hopes of its founders, or rather, to be accurate, I should say, founder, since the other trustees were wholly guided by the initiative of Sidney Webb.

Besides the School, and the Library connected with it, the Trust promoted for many years regular courses of Fabian educational lectures on social and political subjects, such as Socialism, Trade Unionism, Co-operation, Poor Law, Economics, and Economic History. Lecturers were selected with care, and were in some cases given a maintenance allowance during the preparation of their lectures. Then arrangements were made for courses of four lectures each, on what may be called University Extension lines, in four or five centres in one part of the country. For example, in the year 1896-7 180 lectures were given in fifty towns, half of them under the auspices of branches of the I.L.P., and the rest organised by Co-operative Societies, Liberal Associations, Trade Unions, and other bodies. Very careful syllabuses were prepared and widely circulated, and the whole scheme was intended to be educational rather than directly propagandist. The first lecturers engaged were J. Ramsay Macdonald and Miss Enid Stacy, whose premature death, a few years after her marriage to the Rev. Percy Widdrington, was a great loss to the movement. This lecturing was maintained for many years. In 1900, shortly after the creation there of County and District Councils, we experimented upon Ireland, where J. Bruce Glasier and S.D. Shallard gave a number of courses of lectures, without any very obvious results. In 1902 W. Stephen Sanders took over the work, but the fund was coming to an end, and after 1904 subsidised lecturing virtually ceased.

In order to help working-class students who had the desire to study more continuously than by attendance at lectures, correspondence classes were started in the same class of subject as the lectures. A textbook was selected and divided into sections, to each of which an introduction was written, concluding with questions. Written answers were sent in and corrected by the conductor of the class. This went on regularly until 1900, when Ruskin College, Oxford, organised similar classes on a larger scale, and our services were no longer required.

In August, 1896, the triennial International Socialist Workers and Trade Union Congress was held in London, at which the Society was represented by a numerous delegation. The chief business proved to be the expulsion of the Anarchists, who at this period attended these conferences and had to be got rid of before the appointed business could be carried on. The Society prepared an important "Report" for circulation at the Congress, one part of it advocating various reforms, no longer of any special interest, and the other part consisting of a summary of the principles and policy of the Society, drafted by Bernard Shaw in a series of epigrammatic paragraphs. This document, still circulated as Tract 70, is interesting both as a brief and vivid exposition of Fabianism and because it gave rise to another of the long series of fights on the policy of political toleration. The passage chiefly objected to, written, of course, for foreigners, and therefore more detailed than otherwise would be necessary, is as follows:

"Fabian Electoral Tactics.

"The Fabian Society does not claim to be the people of England, or even the Socialist party, and therefore does not seek direct political representation by putting forward Fabian candidates at elections. But it loses no opportunity of influencing elections, and inducing constituencies to select Socialists as their candidates. No person, however, can obtain the support of the Fabian Society or escape its opposition, merely by calling himself a Socialist or Social-Democrat. As there is no Second Ballot in England, frivolous candidatures give great offence and discredit the party in whose name they are undertaken, because any third candidate who is not well supported will not only be beaten himself but may also involve in his defeat the better of the two candidates competing with him. Under such circumstances the Fabian Society throws its weight against the third candidate, whether he calls himself a Socialist or not, in order to secure the victory to the better of the two candidates between whom the contest really lies. But when the third candidate is not only a serious representative of Socialism, but can organise his party well and is likely to poll sufficient votes to make even his defeat a respectable demonstration of the strength and growth of Socialism in the constituency, the Fabian Society supports him resolutely under all circumstances and against all other parties."

This was an extreme statement of our position, because the Society has never, so far as I am aware, taken any action which could be described as "throwing its weight against" a third candidate in a parliamentary election. But it represented our policy as it might have been, if occasion had arisen to carry it to its logical conclusion.

It was opposed, not because it was an inaccurate statement of fact, but because a minority of the Society desired to change the policy it described; and after the Congress was over an influential requisition was got up by J. Ramsay Macdonald, who had been elected to the Executive Committee in 1894, demanding that the tract be withdrawn from circulation. The battle was joined at Clifford's Inn in October, and the insurgents were defeated, after an exciting discussion, by 108 to 33.

There is little to record of the years that followed. Graham Wallas, who had been elected to the London School Board in 1894, resigned his seat on the Executive in 1895; Bernard Shaw became a St. Pancras Vestryman without a contest in 1897, an event rather of literary than political significance, and in 1898 he had a serious illness which kept him out of the movement for nearly two years; whilst at the end of 1899 Sydney Olivier was appointed Colonial Secretary of Jamaica, and spent most of the next fourteen years in the West Indies, latterly as Governor of Jamaica, until 1913, when he was recalled to London to be the Secretary of the Board of Agriculture.

External events put an end to this period of quiescence, and the Society, which was often derisively regarded as expert in the politics of the parish pump, an exponent of "gas and water Socialism," was forced to consider its attitude towards the problems of Imperialism.

War was declared by President Kruger for the South African Republic on October 11th, 1899. Up to this point the whole of the Society, with very few exceptions, had scouted the idea of war. "The grievances alleged, though some of them were real enough, were ludicrously unimportant in comparison with our cognate home grievances. Nobody in his senses would have contemplated a war on their account." But when war had come the situation was entirely altered. The majority of the Society recognised that the British Empire had to win the war, and that no other conclusion to it was possible. Some of us had joined in the protest against the threat of war: but when that protest was fruitless we declined to contest the inevitable. A large section of the Liberal Party and nearly all other Socialists took another view. They appeared to believe, and some of them even hoped, that the Boers might be successful and the British army be driven to the sea. The I.L.P. regarded the war as a typical case of the then accepted theory of Socialism that war is always instigated by capitalists for the purpose of obtaining profits. They opposed every step in the prosecution of the campaign, and criticised every action of the British authorities.

In this matter the left and right wings of the Fabians joined hands in opposition to the centre. Members who came into the movement when Marxism was supreme, like Walter Crane, those who worked largely with the I.L.P., such as J. Ramsay Macdonald, S.G. Hobson, and G.N. Barnes (later M.P. and Chairman of the Labour Party), were joined by others who were then associated with the Liberals, such as Dr. F. Lawson Dodd, Will Crooks (later Labour M.P.), Clement Edwards (later Liberal M.P.), and Dr. John Clifford. On the other side were the older leaders of the Society, who took the view that the members had come together for the purpose of promoting Socialism, that the question at issue was one "which Socialism cannot solve and does not touch," and that whilst each member was entitled to hold and work for his own opinion, it was not necessary for the Society in its corporate capacity to adopt a formal policy with the result of excluding the large minority which would have objected to whatever decision was arrived at.

The first round in the contest was at a business meeting on October 13th, 1899, when on the advice of the Executive the members present rejected a motion of urgency for the discussion of a resolution expressing sympathy with the Boers.

It was however agreed that the matter could not end thus, and a members' meeting was fixed for December 8th, at Clifford's Inn Hall, when S.G. Hobson moved a long resolution declaring it essential that the attitude of the Society in regard to the war should be clearly asserted, and concluding: "The Fabian Society therefore formally dissociates itself from the Imperialism of Capitalism and vainglorious Nationalism and pledges itself to support the expansion of the Empire only in so far as it may be compatible with the expansion of that higher social organisation which this Society was founded to promote."

Bernard Shaw, on behalf of the Executive Committee, moved a long reasoned amendment declaring that a parliamentary vote was not worth fighting about, demanding that at the conclusion of the war measures be taken for securing the value of the Transvaal mines for the public, and that the interests of the miners be safeguarded. The amendment was barely relevant to the issue, and notwithstanding influential support it was defeated by 58 to 27. Thereupon the "previous question" was moved and carried by 59 to 50. This inconclusive result revealed a great diversity of opinion in the Society, and the Executive Committee, for the first and, so far, the only time, availed itself of the rule which authorised it to submit any question to a postal referendum of all the members.

The question submitted in February, 1900, was this: "Are you in favour of an official pronouncement being made now by the Fabian Society on Imperialism in relation to the War?" and on the paper published in the "News" were printed four reasons on one side and five on the other, drafted by those members of the Executive who advocated each policy. On the one hand it was argued that the Society should resist aggressive capitalism and militarism, thus putting itself into line with international socialism, and that expenditure on the war would postpone social reform. On the other it was contended that the question was outside the province of the Society, that a resolution by the Society would carry no weight, would not stop the war, and might have a serious effect on the solidarity of the Society itself. The vote excited great interest: an appeal to the electorate to vote Yes, worded with much moderation, was issued by Walter Crane, S.G. Hobson, Charles Charrington, F. Lawson Dodd, J. Frederick Green, George N. Barnes, Will Crooks, Henry S. Salt, Dr. John Clifford, Mrs. Mallet, Clement Edwards, Mrs. J.R. Macdonald and others; to which a reply was sent, signed only by members of the Executive, Bernard Shaw, Sidney Webb, Hubert Bland, J.F. Oakeshott, H.W. Macrosty and one or two others. Finally a rejoinder by the signatories of the first circular was issued in the course of the poll which extended over nearly a month. The membership at the time was about 800, of whom 50 lived abroad, and in all only 476 votes were cast, 217 in favour of a pronouncement and 259 against.

It was said at the time, and has constantly been alleged since, that the Society had voted its approval of the South African War and had supported imperialist aggression and anti-democratic militarism. As will be seen from the foregoing, no such statement is correct. A vote on the policy of the Government would have given an overwhelming adverse majority, but it would have destroyed the Society. In early days we had drawn a clear line between Socialism and politics: we had put on one side such problems as Home Rule and Church Disestablishment as of the nature of red herrings, matters of no real importance in comparison with the economic enfranchisement which we advocated. In the early eighties Parliament spent futile and fruitless months discussing whether Mr. Bradlaugh should take the oath, and whether an extension of the franchise should or should not be accompanied by redistribution. We wanted to make the working classes pay less attention to these party questions and more attention to their own social conditions. We thought, or at any rate said, that the Liberal and Conservative leaders kept the party ball rolling in order to distract the workers from the iniquity of the distribution of wealth. We insisted that Socialism was an economic doctrine, and had nothing to do with other problems. Later on we realised that the form of government is scarcely less important than its content: that the unit of administration, whether imperial, national, or local, is germane to the question of the services to be administered; that if the governmental machine is to be used for industry, that machine must be modern and efficient: and that in fact no clear line of distinction can be drawn between the problems of constitutional structure which concern Socialism and those, if any, which do not concern it. In the case of the South African war it was mainly the instinct of self-preservation that actuated us; it is certain that any other decision would have destroyed the Society. The passions of that period were extraordinarily bitter. The Pro-Boers were mobbed and howled down, their actions were misrepresented, and their motives disparaged: they retaliated by accusing the British troops of incredible atrocities, by rejoicing over every disaster which befell our arms, and by prophesying all sorts of calamities however the war ended. There was never any question of the Society issuing a pronouncement justifying the war. Only a very few of our members went as far as that. But many others, all or nearly all who were now beginning to be called the "old gang," on whom from first to last the initiative and stability of the Society has depended, would have declined to be associated with what they regarded as the anti-patriotic excesses of certain of the Liberals, and would have resigned their membership, or at any rate their official positions in the Society, had it adopted at that time the same policy as the I.L.P. Happily tolerance prevailed, and although an attempt was made to get up a big secession, only about fifteen members resigned in a group when the result of the poll was declared. These, however, included a few important names, J. Ramsay Macdonald and J. Frederick Green, of the Executive Committee, George N. Barnes and Pete Curran, future Labour Members of Parliament, Walter Crane, H.S. Salt, Mrs. J.R. Macdonald, and Mrs. Pankhurst.

At the election of the Executive Committee in April, 1900, the Society by another vote confirmed the previous decision. All the old members were re-elected, and those of the majority party polled the heaviest votes. The two seats vacated by resignation were filled by "Pro-Boers," and the only new candidate who supported the majority was defeated. It was clear, therefore, that the voting was not strictly on party lines—one of the opposition, Charles Charrington, was fourth on the poll—but that the Society as a whole approved of the non-committal policy. The Executive Committee had been elected since 1894 by a postal ballot of the whole Society, and on this occasion 509 members, over 62 per cent of the whole, recorded their votes.

The Executive had resolved at the beginning of the war to issue a tract on Imperialism, and at the Annual Meeting in May, 1900, a resolution was passed that it prepare for submission to the members "a constructive criticism from the Socialist standpoint of the actions and programmes of the various political parties."

Needless to say, Bernard Shaw undertook the difficult job, for at this period all the official pronouncements of the Executive were drafted by him. At the beginning of September it was announced as nearly ready, and later in the month a proof was sent to every member for criticism, and a meeting was called for the 25th to discuss it. This was the extreme example of the practice at that time habitual, of inviting the co-operation of every member in our publications. No less than 134 members returned amended proofs or wrote letters of criticism; and it is recorded that only one of these was opposed to the whole thing, whilst only nine preferred to have no manifesto at all; and another nine objected to material portions. The great majority were cordial in approval.

Bernard Shaw is fond of posing as the most conceited of persons, but those who have had to do with him in literary matters are aware that no pose was ever more preposterous. When he has acted as the literary expert of the Fabian Society he has considered every criticism with unruffled courtesy, and dealt with the many fools who always find their way into extreme parties, not according to their folly, but with the careful consideration properly accorded to eminent wisdom. The business of examining over a hundred marked proofs of a document of 20,000 words, every line of which was more or less controversial, was an immense one, but the author gave every criticism its proper weight, and accepted every useful amendment. Then came the meeting. It was held at Clifford's Inn, and between 130 and 140 members were present, each of whom was entitled to move any amendment on any of the 20,000 words, or any addition to or deletion of them. Nearly three hours were occupied partly in discussing the controversial portion and partly with the general question of publication. Only eighteen voted for omitting the part about Imperialism, and the minority against the publication numbered no more than fourteen. By this time the controversy over the war had reached an intensity which those who cannot recollect it will find difficult to believe, and nobody but the author could have written an effective document on the war so skilfully as to satisfy the great majority of the supporters of both parties in the Society. Bernard Shaw has accomplished many difficult feats, but none of them, in my opinion, excels that of drafting for the Society and carrying through the manifesto called "Fabianism and the Empire."

It was published as a shilling volume by Grant Richards, and although it was widely and favourably noticed in the Press the sales were only moderate, just over 2000 copies to the end of the year. Some time later the Society purchased the remainder of 1500 copies at 1d. and since sold them at prices, rising as the stock declined, up to five shillings a copy!

The theme of the manifesto is the overriding claim of efficiency not only in our own government, and in our empire, but throughout the world. The earth belongs to mankind, and the only valid moral right to national as well as individual possession is that the occupier is making adequate use of it for the benefit of the world community. "The problem before us is how the world can be ordered by Great Powers of practically international extent.... The partition of the greater part of the globe among such powers is, as a matter of fact that must be faced approvingly or deploringly, now only a question of time" (p. 3). "The notion that a nation has a right to do what it pleases with its own territory, without reference to the interests of the rest of the world is no more tenable from the International Socialist point of view — that is, from the point of view of the twentieth century — than the notion that a landlord has a right to do what he likes with his estate without reference to the interests of his neighbours.... [In China] we are asserting and enforcing international rights of travel and trade. But the right to trade is a very comprehensive one: it involves a right to insist on a settled government which can keep the peace and enforce agreements. When a native government of this order is impossible, the foreign trading power must set one up" (pp. 44-5). "The value of a State to the world lies in the quality of its civilisation, not in the magnitude of its armaments.... There is therefore no question of the steam-rollering of little States because they are little, any more than of their maintenance in deference to romantic nationalism. The State which obstructs international civilisation will have to go, be it big or little. That which advances it should be defended by all the Western Powers. Thus huge China and little Monaco may share the same fate, little Switzerland and the vast United States the same fortune" (p. 46).

As for South Africa, "however ignorantly [our] politicians may argue about it, reviling one another from the one side as brigands, and defending themselves from the other with quibbles about waste-paper treaties and childish slanders against a brave enemy, the fact remains that a Great Power, consciously or unconsciously, must govern in the interests of civilisation as a whole; and it is not to those interests that such mighty forces as gold-fields, and the formidable armaments that can be built upon them, should be wielded irresponsibly by small communities of frontiersmen. Theoretically they should be internationalised, not British-Imperialised; but until the Federation of the World becomes an accomplished fact we must accept the most responsible Imperial federations available as a substitute for it" (pp. 23-4).

As however the Manifesto was designed for the general election, this theme was only sketched, and the greater part was occupied with matters of a more immediately practicable character. The proposed partition of China at that time seemed imminent, and our attention had been called to the efficiency of the German State organisation of foreign trade in comparison with the *laissez-faire* policy which dominated our Foreign Office. We regarded our overseas trade as a national asset, and urged that the consular service should be revolutionised. "Any person who thinks this application of Socialism to foreign trade through the consular system impossible also thinks the survival of his country in the age of the Powers impossible. No German thinks it impossible. If he has not already achieved it, he intends to" (pp. 10, 11). We must "have in every foreign market an organ of commercially disinterested industrial intelligence. A developed consulate would be such an organ." "The consulate could itself act as broker, if necessary, and have a revenue from commissions, of which, however, the salaries of its officials should be strictly independent" (pp. 10 and 8).

The present army should be replaced "by giving to the whole male population an effective training in the use of arms without removing them from civil life. This can be done without conscription or barrack life" by extending the half-time system to the age of 21 and training the young men in the other half. From the millions of men thus trained "we could obtain by voluntary enlistment a picked professional force of engineers, artillery, and cavalry, and as large a garrison for outlying provinces as we chose to pay for, if we made it attractive by the following reforms": full civil rights, a living wage, adequate superannuation after long service, and salaries for officers on the civil scale. The other reforms advocated included a minimum wage for labour, grants in aid for housing, freedom for municipal trading, municipal public-houses, and reorganisation of the machinery of education, as explained later. "The moral of it all is that what the British Empire wants most urgently in its government is not Conservatism, not Liberalism, not Imperialism, but brains and political science" (p. 93).

Chapter VIII   Education: 1902-5, and the Labour Party: 1900-15

Housing – "The Education muddle and the way out" – Supporting the Conservatives – The Education Acts of 1902 and 1903--Feeding School Children – The Labour Representation Committee formed – The Fabian Election Fund – Will Crooks elected in 1910--A Fabian Cabinet Minister – Resignation of Graham Wallas – The younger generation: H.W. Macrosty, J.F. Oakeshott, John W. Martin – Municipal Drink Trade – Tariff Reform – The Decline of the Birth-rate.

The controversy described in the preceding chapter was not the only business that occupied the Society at the period of the South African War.

Amongst minor affairs was a change of premises. The office first taken, in 1891, was at 276 Strand, in the island at that time formed by Holywell Street which ran between the churches of St. Clement Danes and St. Martin's in the Fields. At the end of 1899 the London County Council acquired the property for the Kingsway and Aldwych clearance scheme, and we found new quarters in a basement at . Clement's Inn, a pleasant couple of rooms, with plenty of light, though sometimes maliciously misdescribed as a cellar. At the end of 1908 we removed into three much more spacious rooms at the same address, also in "a dismal basement," where we remained until in 1914 the Society rented a house at 25 Tothill Street, Westminster.

Another undertaking was a conference on Housing. Although the first public effort of the Society was its conference at South Place Chapel in 1886, this particular form of propaganda has never commended itself to the Executive, chiefly no doubt because conferences, to which numerous representative persons are invited, are most useful for promoting moderate reforms which have already made themselves acceptable to the members and officials of local governing bodies. Such reforms the Fabian Society does not regard as its special business; it prefers to pioneer; it is true that it uses its machinery for spreading a knowledge of local government in all its forms, but that is mainly a matter of office routine.

However, for once we took up an already popular proposal. The Housing of the Working Classes Act of 1890 was an admirable measure, but it was hedged about with obstacles which rendered it very difficult to work in urban areas and virtually useless in rural districts. We had drafted an amending Bill for rural districts in 1895, which was read a first time in the House of Commons on the day of the vote on the supply of cordite, when the defeat of the Liberal Government led to the dissolution of Parliament.

The Act of 1890 was singular in one respect. Part III was headed "Working-Class Lodging Houses," and was drafted accordingly, but the definition of lodging-houses was made to include cottages with not more than half an acre of garden, thus enabling houses to be provided by local authorities in town and country, apart from clearances of insanitary areas. For years this definition was overlooked, and very few people were aware that cottages could be built in rural districts by the Guardians, and later by Rural District Councils. Our Leaflet No. 63, "Parish Council Cottages," issued in 1895, was almost the first publication drawing attention to the subject, and with one exception no use was made of these powers of the Act in rural districts before that year. Our Tract 76, "Houses for the People," published in 1897, explained the Act in simple language, and was widely circulated.

In 1900 an amending Act, chiefly to simplify procedure in rural districts, was promised by the Government; and the conference we called was intended to agitate for widening its scope and strengthening its provisions. The papers, read by Clement Edwards (afterwards M.P.), Miss Constance Cochrane, Alderman Thompson, and others, were first discussed at a preliminary private meeting in December, and then submitted to the Conference, which was held on March 1st, the day following the Conference at which the Labour Party was established. By choosing this date we secured a large number of delegates from Trade Unions, and these were reinforced by numerous delegates from Vestries and other local authorities, altogether numbering about 400. At the close of the proceedings a National Committee was formed with headquarters at the Fabian Office, which had however only a short career. The Conference papers were printed as a bulky penny tract, "The House Famine and How to Relieve It," which rapidly went through two editions. We also published "Cottage Plans and Common Sense," by Raymond Unwin, which describes how cottages should be built—an anticipation of garden suburbs and town-planning—and a compilation of everything which Parish Councils had done and could do, including housing, prepared by Sidney Webb and called "Five Years' Fruits of the Parish Councils Act," which in 1908 was revised and reissued as "Parish Councils and Village Life." A speech by W.C. Steadman, M.P., who was a member of the Society, was printed under the title "Overcrowding and Its Remedy." Our agitation was not without results. The amending Acts of 1900, 1903, and 1909 have done much to remove the unnecessary administrative complexities of the Act of 1890, but in fact the problem is still unsolved, and the scandalous character of our housing, both urban and rural, remains perhaps the blackest blot in the record of British civilisation.

The Society had always been concerned in public education. Its first electoral success was when Mrs. Besant and the Rev. Stewart Headlam were elected to the London School Board in 1888, and except for one interval of three years Mr. Headlam has sat on the School Board and its successor, the London County Council, ever since. Sidney Webb was Chairman or Vice-Chairman of the L.C.C. Technical Education Board from its foundation in 1893, almost continuously until the Board came to an end in 1904, after the London Education Act. Graham Wallas was elected to the School Board in 1894, and from 1897 onwards was Chairman of the School Management Committee; he had been re-elected in 1900, and was therefore filling the most important administrative position on the Board when the Education question was before the Society.

The educational scheme of the Society was not, however, the joint production of its experts. It was entirely the work of Sidney Webb. Headlam and Wallas, and the members who took part, contributed their share as critics, but as critics only, and for the most part as hostile critics. It was in part a struggle between the County Councils and the School Boards and in part a controversy over the denominational schools. Wallas opposed our proposals in the main because he regarded them as too favourable to sectarian education: Headlam was against them on both issues. They put up a vigorous fight, but they were beaten every time in the Society, as the defenders of School Boards were beaten ultimately in Parliament and in the country.

The first step in the controversy was taken in May, 1899, when a Members' Meeting was held to discuss "The Education Muddle and the Way Out," in the form of sixteen resolutions, six on "General Principles" and the remainder on "Immediate Practicable Proposals." These were introduced by Webb, and the "General Principles," advocating the transfer of education to the local government authority and the abolition of School Boards, were adopted. Amendments by Graham Wallas were defeated by large majorities, and the discussion on the second part, the immediately practicable proposals, was adjourned.

At the adjourned meeting in November, 1899, the resolutions were put aside and a draft tract was submitted. Graham Wallas again led the opposition, which was always unsuccessful, though serious shortcomings in the proposals were revealed and it was agreed to meet the criticisms wherever possible. Finally it was decided to appoint a Revision Committee, on which Wallas was placed. Thirteen months passed before the scheme came before the Society again; in December the tract as amended was submitted, and this time the chief critic was Mr. Headlam. On the main question of principle he found only one supporter, and with minor amendments the scheme was adopted.

It is unnecessary to describe the Fabian plan, because it is substantially the system of administration, established by the Act of 1902, under which present-day education is organised. The main difference is that we presented a revolutionary proposal in an extremely moderate form and Mr. Arthur Balfour found himself able to carry out our principles more thoroughly than we thought practically possible. Our tract advocated the abolition of all School

Boards, but anticipated, incorrectly, that those of the twenty or thirty largest cities would be too strong to be destroyed: and whilst insisting that the public must find all the money required to keep the voluntary schools in full efficiency, we only proposed that this should take the form of a large grant by County Councils and County Boroughs, whilst Mr. Balfour was able to make the Councils shoulder the cost.

How far the draughtsmen of the Bill were influenced by the Fabian scheme cannot here be estimated, but the authorities at Whitehall were so anxious to see it that they were supplied with proofs before publication; and the tract when published was greedily devoured by perplexed M.P.'s.

It must be recollected that the whole complex machinery of educational administration was in the melting-pot, and nobody knew what was to come out of it. It had been assumed by nearly everybody that education was a department of local government which demanded for its management a special class of representatives. The Liberal Party was attached to School Boards, because their creation had been one of the great party victories of Mr. Gladstone's greatest Government, because they embodied a triumph over the Church and the virtual establishment of nonconformity in control of half the elementary schools of the country. Socialists and the vague labour section took the same view partly because they believed theoretically in direct election for all purposes and partly because the cumulative vote, intended to secure representation to minorities, gave them better chances of success at the polls than they then had in any other local election. The Board schools, with ample funds derived from the rates, were far better than the so-called voluntary schools; but more than half the children of the nation were educated in these schools, under-staffed, ill-equipped, and on the average in all respects inefficient. Every year that passed turned out thus its quota of poorly educated children. Something had to be done at once to provide more money for these inferior schools. It might be better that they should be abolished and State schools everywhere supplied, but this was a counsel of perfection, and there was no time to wait for it. Then again the distinction between elementary education for the poor, managed by School Boards and by the voluntary school authorities, and other education controlled and subsidised by Town and County Councils, was disastrous, the more so since a recent legal decision (the Cockerton case) had restricted the limits of School Board education more narrowly than ever.

All sorts of projects might have been proposed for solving these complex difficulties, projects drafted in the interests of the Church or the Nonconformists, the voluntary schools or the schools of the local authorities: but, in fact, the scheme proposed by Mr. Balfour followed almost precisely the lines laid down in our tract, which was published in January, 1901, and of which 20,000 copies were quickly circulated.

At the Annual Meeting in May, 1901, a resolution was adopted, in spite of the vigorous opposition of Mr. Headlam, welcoming the Government Bill and suggesting various amendments to it. This Bill was withdrawn, to be reintroduced a year later as the Education Bill, 1902, which ultimately became law. This measure was considered at a meeting in May, 1902, and a long series of resolutions welcoming the Bill and advocating amendments on eighteen different points was carried in spite of vigorous opposition. Nearly all these amendments, the chief of which was directed to making the Bill compulsory where it was drafted as optional, were embodied in the Act.

Our support of the Conservative Government in their education policy caused much surprise and attracted not a little attention. We had been suspected by other Socialists, not without excuse, of intrigues with the Liberals, and our attack on that party in 1893 was made exclusively in the interests of Labour. Now when Liberals and Labour were united in denouncing the Government, when Nonconformists who had deserted Liberalism on the Home Rule issue were returning in thousands to their old party, the Fabians, alone amongst progressives (except of course the Irish, who were keen to save the Roman Catholic schools), supported the Government in what was popularly regarded as a reactionary policy. Time has vindicated our judgment. The theological squabbles which occupied so much of the energies of the School Boards are now forgotten because the rival sects are no longer represented on the Education Authorities, that is, the town and county councils. Education has been secularised in the sense that it is no longer governed by clerics, and though some Liberals now desire to carry Mr. Balfour's policy still further, the Liberal Party in its ten years of office has never been able to affect any further change.

The Act of 1902 did not apply to London, and in the great province ruled by its County Council the case for maintaining the separate existence of the School Board was stronger than anywhere else. The London County Council itself was unwilling to undertake elementary education, and the School Board, like all other bodies in such circumstances, vehemently objected to its own dissolution. The Board was efficient; its schools were excellent; there was no evidence that the already overburdened County Council could properly carry on the work. On the other hand, the Fabian Society was in a stronger position. The Chairman of the Technical Education Board was something more than a self-constituted authority on the organisation of education: and the other members of the Society were engaged on a contest on their home ground. Into the details of the resolutions submitted to the Fabian Society outlining a plan for London education it is needless now to enter, except to say that Graham Wallas on this issue supported, without enthusiasm, the policy of the Society. Mr. Balfour made no fewer than three attempts to solve the problem, each time approaching more nearly to the plan prepared by the Fabian Society. On the third and eventually successful Bill thirteen amendments were formulated by the Society, eleven of which were adopted by the House of Commons, and finally, to quote our Annual Report, "the Act only departed from our plan by giving to the Borough Councils the appointment of two-thirds of the managers of provided schools, while we desired the proportion to be one-half, and omitting a proposal that the Education Authority should have compulsory powers to acquire sites for schools other than elementary."

On the County Council itself, which was strongly opposed to the Bill, Mr. Webb conducted a skilful and successful campaign to defeat a policy of passive resistance which might have led to endless difficulties. But that is outside the history of the Fabian Society.

It should be added that the Society did not content itself with merely passing resolutions. All these documents were printed by thousands and posted to members of Parliament and of education authorities up and down the country: our members incessantly lectured and debated at Liberal Associations and Clubs, and indefatigably worked the London and Provincial presses; none of the resources of skilful propagandists was neglected which might shake the opposition to the Bills, or convince some of the Liberal and Labour opponents that for once at any rate a good thing might come from the Conservative Party.

The transfer of the control of all elementary schools to the local authorities rendered at last possible the public feeding of school children, long before advocated by the Social Democratic Federation. This had hitherto been regarded by the Fabian Society as impracticable; though an eloquent and often quoted passage in Graham Wallas's contribution to "Fabian Essays" describes the schools of the future with "associated meals [served] on tables spread with flowers, in halls surrounded with beautiful pictures, or even, as John Milton proposed, filled with the sound of music." Our contribution towards this ideal was Tract No. 120, "After Bread Education: a Plan for the State Feeding of School Children," published in 1905, one of the few tracts for which Hubert Bland was largely responsible, which advocated a reform carried into law a year later.

In 1893, and even before, the Fabian Society had urged the Trade Unionists to form a Labour Party of their own, and earlier in the same year the Independent Labour Party had been founded which was originally intended to achieve the object indicated by its name, but which quickly became a purely Socialist society. It carried on a vigorous and successful propaganda amongst Trade Unionists, with the result that in 1899 the Trade Union Congress passed a resolution directing its Parliamentary Committee, in co-operation with the Socialist Societies, to call a conference in order "to devise ways and means for securing an increased number of Labour members in the next Parliament." In accordance with this resolution the Society was invited to appoint two representatives to meet the delegates of the Parliamentary Committee and of the two other Socialist organisations. Bernard Shaw and myself were appointed, and we took part in the business of arranging for the Conference. This was held on the last two days of February, 1900, and I was appointed the one delegate to which the Society was by its numbers entitled. The "Labour Representation Committee" was duly formed, and it was decided that the Executive Committee of twelve should include one elected by the Fabian Society. This Committee was constituted then and there, and, as "Fabian News" reports, "Edward R. Pease provisionally appointed himself, as the only Fabian delegate, to be on the Executive Committee, and the Executive Committee has since confirmed the appointment." This little comedy was carried on for some years. The Fabian Society was only entitled to send one delegate to the annual conference, but that delegate had the right of electing one member to the Executive Committee, and I was appointed by my Committee to serve in both capacities. But the incident embodies a moral. The Trade Unionists on the Committee represented in the earlier years about 100,000 members each: I then represented some 700. But although it was often proposed to amend the constitution by giving every vote an equal value, the Trade Union leaders always defended the over-representation of the Socialists (the I.L.P. were also over-represented, though their case was not so extreme) partly because the Labour Representation Committee was founded as a federation of Socialists and Trade Unionists, and partly because Socialist Societies, consisting exclusively of persons keenly concerned in politics, were entitled to larger representation per head of membership than Unions which were primarily non-political. But when we remember how attractive to the average man are broad generalisations like "one vote one value," and how plausible a case could be made out against discrimination in favour of Socialist Societies, it has always seemed to me a remarkable example of the practical common sense of organised labour that the old constitution has been preserved, in fact though not precisely in form, to the present day. By the present constitution the "Socialist Section" elects three members to the Executive from nominations sent in advance; but as the I.L.P. always makes two nominations, and the Fabian Society one, the alteration of the rule has not in fact made any change, and the over-representation of this section is of course undiminished.

Six months after the Labour Representation Committee was formed the Society adopted a project drafted by Mr. S.G. Hobson for a Labour Members' Guarantee Fund, and circulated it amongst the Unions affiliated to the Committee. The proposal was submitted by its author on behalf of the Society to the Labour Representation Conference of 1901, but an amendment both approving of the scheme and declaring that the time was not ripe for it was carried. A year later however the Conference unanimously agreed to establish its Parliamentary Fund by which salaries for their M.P.'s were provided until Parliament itself undertook the business.

For several years after this the Fabian Society did not greatly concern itself with the Labour Party. I attended the Annual Conferences and took a regular part in the work of the Executive Committee, but my colleagues of the Fabian Society as a whole showed little interest in the new body. In a sense, it was not in our line. Its object was to promote Labour Representation in Parliament, and the Fabian Society had never run, and had never intended to run, candidates for Parliament or for any local authority. We had made appeals for election funds on a good many occasions and had succeeded once or twice in collecting substantial sums, but this was a very different matter from accepting responsibility for a candidate and his election expenses. Therefore, for a good while, we remained in a position of benevolent passivity.

The Labour Representation Committee was founded as a Group, not as a Party, and one of the two members elected under its auspices at the General Election of 1900 ran as a Liberal. In 1903 it transformed itself into a Party, and then began the somewhat strange anomaly that the Fabian Society as a whole was affiliated to the Labour Party, whilst some of its members were Liberal Members of Parliament. It is true that the Trade Unions affiliated to the party were in the same position: their members also were sometimes official Liberals and even Liberal M.P.'s. The Labour Party itself never complained of the anomaly in the position of the Society or questioned its collective loyalty. And the Liberals in our Society never took any action hostile to the Labour Party, or indeed, so far as I know, supported any of the proposals occasionally made that we should disaffiliate from it. These proposals always came from "Fabian reformers," the younger men who wanted to create a revolution in the Society. And so little was their policy matured that in several cases the same member first tried to get the Society to expel all members who worked with any party other than the Labour Party, and a short time later moved that the Society should leave the Labour Party altogether. Or perhaps it was the other way round. Logical consistency is usually incompatible with political success: compromise runs smooth, whilst principle jams. But the lesser sort of critic, on the look out for a grievance, can always apply a principle to a compromise, point out that it does not fit, and that difficulties may arise. In the case in question they have in fact rarely arisen, and such as have occurred have been easily surmounted. It is not necessary to record here all the proposals put forward from time to time that the Society should disaffiliate from the Labour Party, or on the other hand, that it should expel, directly or indirectly, all members who did not confine their political activities to co-operating with the Labour Party. It may be assumed that one or other of these proposals was made every few years after the Labour Party was constituted, and that in every case it was defeated, as a rule, by a substantial majority.

The Labour Party won three remarkable victories in the period between the General Election of 1900 and that of 1906. In 1902 Mr. David Shackleton was returned unopposed for a Liberal seat, the Clitheroe Division of Lancashire; in 1903 Mr. (now the Right Hon.)

Will Crooks, an old member of our Society, captured Woolwich from the Conservatives by a majority of 3229, amidst a scene of enthusiasm which none who were present will ever forget: and five months later Mr. (now the Right Hon.) Arthur Henderson, who later became a member of our Society, beat both Liberal and Tory opponents at the Barnard Castle Division of Durham.

When the election campaign of 1906 began the Labour Party put fifty candidates into the field and succeeded in carrying no fewer than twenty-nine of them, whilst another joined the party after his election. Four of these were members of the Fabian Society, and in addition three Fabians were successful as Liberals, including Percy Alden, then a member of our Executive Committee.

Whilst the election was in progress Mr. H.G. Wells began the Fabian reform movement which is described in the next chapter. At that time he did not bring the Labour Party into his scheme of reconstruction, but some of the members of his Committee were then ardent adherents of that party, and they persuaded his Committee to report in favour of the Society's choosing "in harmonious co-operation with other Socialist and Labour bodies, Parliamentary Candidates of its own. Constituencies for such candidates should be selected, a special election fund raised and election campaigns organised."

The result was that a resolution proposed by the Executive Committee was carried early in March, 1907, directing the appointment of a Committee to report on "the best means of promoting local Socialist societies of the Fabian type with the object of increasing Socialist representation in Parliament as a party co-operating as far as possible with the Labour Party whilst remaining independent of that and of all other Parties."

This, it will be observed, is a different proposition, and one which resulted in a lot of talk and nothing else. Bernard Shaw had the idea that there might be county constituencies in the South of England, where independent middle-class Socialists could win when Labour candidates had no chance. No such constituency has ever been discovered and the Fabian scheme has never even begun to be realised.

In January, 1908, the Committee's Report was considered and adopted, the important item being the decision to send a circular to every member inviting promises to an election fund of at least £5,000, contributions to be spread over five years. This ultimately resulted in promises amounting to £2637 — a much larger sum than the Society had ever had at its command — and with this substantial fund in prospect the Society was in a position to begin the business of electioneering.

A favourable opportunity soon presented itself. A vacancy at the little town of Taunton was not to be fought by the Liberals, while the Conservative candidate, the Hon. W. (now Viscount) Peel, was a London County Councillor, bitterly opposed even to the mild collectivism of the London Progressives. Frank Smith, a member both of the Society and the London County Council, was willing to fight, the Labour Party Executive cordially approved, and the members promptly paid up the first instalment of their promises. The election cost £316, of which the Society paid £275, and although our candidate was beaten by 1976 votes to 1085, the result was not contrary to our anticipations.

During 1909 the Executive Committee resolved to run two candidates, both already nominated by the I.L.P., who willingly transferred to us the responsibility for their election expenses. W. Stephen Sanders had been third on the poll out of six candidates who fought in 1906 for the two seats at Portsmouth, and as he had polled 8172 votes, more than either Conservative, it was reasonably hoped that the Liberals would leave one of the seats to him. Harry Snell at Huddersfield was opposing both parties, but had a fair chance of winning. At the General Election of January, 1910, neither of these candidates was successful, Sanders, opposed by Lord Charles Beresford with an irresistible shipbuilding programme, only obtaining 3529 votes, whilst at Huddersfield Snell was second on the poll, but 1472 behind the Liberal. Elsewhere, however, the members of the Society did well, no less than eight securing seats, four for the Labour Party and four as Liberals.

In December, 1910, we won our first electoral victory. Will Crooks had lost his seat at Woolwich in January by 295 votes. It was decided to take over his candidature from the Coopers' Union, a very small society which only nominally financed it, and also to support Harry Snell again at Huddersfield. Will Crooks was victorious by 236 votes, but Harry Snell failed to reduce the Liberal majority. Elsewhere members of the Society were very successful. In all eight secured seats for the Labour Party and four for the Liberals, amongst the latter Mr. (now Sir) L.G. Chiozza Money, then a member of the Executive Committee.

This brings the electoral record of the Society up to the present time, except that it should be mentioned that Mr. Arthur Henderson, M.P., who became a member of the Society in 1912, was in 1915 both Secretary of the Labour Party Executive and Chairman of the party in the House of Commons, until he relinquished the latter position on joining the Coalition Cabinet as Minister for Education, being thus actually the first member of a Socialist society to attain Cabinet rank in this country during his membership.

During these later years the Fabian Society with its increased numbers was entitled to several delegates at the annual conference of the Labour Party, and it frequently took part in the business by putting motions or amendments on the agenda paper. All talk of forming a Fabian Socialist Party had died away, and the Executive Committee had shown itself far more appreciative of the importance of the Labour Party than in earlier years. I continued to represent the Society on the Executive Committee until the end of 1913, when I retired, and the new General Secretary, W. Stephen Sanders, took my place. When in December, 1915, he accepted a commission for the period of the war, as a recruiting officer, Sidney Webb was appointed to fill the vacancy.

The account of the part taken by the Society in the work of the Labour Party has carried us far beyond the period previously described, and a short space must now be devoted to the years which intervened between the Education episode and the outburst of activity to be described in the next chapter.

Social progress advances in waves, and outbursts of energy are always succeeded by depressions. Up to 1899 the Society slowly grew in membership until this reached 861. Then it slowly declined to 730 in 1904. This was symptomatic of a general lack of interest in Socialism. The lectures and meetings were poorly attended, and the really important debates which decided our educational policy were conducted by only a few dozen members. Twenty years had passed since the Society was founded. Of the Essayists Bernard Shaw, Sidney Webb, Hubert Bland, and when in England, Sydney Olivier were still leaders of the Society, and so until January, 1904, was Graham Wallas, who then resigned his membership on account of his disagreement with the tract on Tariff Reform, but really, as his letter published in "Fabian News" indicated, because in the long controversy over education policy he had found himself constantly in the position of a hostile critic. It should be added that his resignation has been followed by none of those personal and political disagreements which so commonly accompany the severance of old associations. Mr. Wallas has remained a Fabian in all except name. His friendship with his old colleagues has been unbroken, and he has always been willing to assist the Society out of his abundant stores of special knowledge both by lecturing at its meetings and by taking part in conferences and even by attending quite small meetings of special groups.

In all these years a large number of younger members had come forward, none of them of quite the same calibre as the Essayists, but many of them contributing much to the sum total of the Society's influence. Of these perhaps the most active was Henry W. Macrosty, who sat on the Executive from 1895 till 1907, when he retired on account of the pressure of official duties. During and indeed before his period of office Mr. Macrosty was constantly engaged in research and writing for the Society. He prepared the Eight Hours Bill which approached nearest to practicability (Tract 48, "Eight Hours by Law," 1893); in 1898 he wrote for the Society "State Arbitration and the Living Wage" (Tract 83); in 1899, Tract 88, "The Growth of Monopoly in English Industry"; in 1905 "The Revival of Agriculture, a national policy for Great Britain," the last named an extraordinarily farsighted anticipation of the chief reforms which were advocated with such vigour by the Liberal Party, and indeed by all parties in the years preceding the great war. In the same year his "State Control of Trusts" was published as Tract 124. As I have before explained, a great part of the published work of the Society has been prepared co-operatively, and in this process Mr. Macrosty always took an active part. He had a considerable share in drafting the innumerable documents issued in connection with the education controversy, and indeed participated in all the activities of the Executive until his retirement.

Scarcely less active was Joseph F. Oakeshott, who has been already mentioned in connection with the Fellowship of the New Life. He joined the Executive when it was first enlarged in 1890, and sat until 1902. A Somerset House official, like Macrosty, he was strong on statistics, and for many years he undertook the constant revisions of the figures of national income, in the various editions of our "Facts for Socialists."

His "Democratic Budget" (Tract 39) was our first attempt to apply Socialism to taxation: and his "Humanising of the Poor Law" (Tract

54), published in 1894, set out the policy which in recent years has been widely adopted by the better Boards of Guardians.

John W. Martin sat on the Executive from 1894 to 1899, wrote Tract No. 52, "State Education at Home and Abroad" (1894), and did a lot of valuable lecturing, both here and in America, where he married the leading exponent of Fabianism and editor of a monthly called "The American Fabian," and, settling in New York, has since, under the name of John Martin, played a considerable part in the educational and progressive politics of his adopted city.

I will conclude this chapter with a short account of some of the applications of Socialism to particular problems which were studied by the Society in or about this period of its history.

In 1897 and 1898 a good deal of time was devoted to working out a scheme for the municipalisation of the Drink Trade. This was before the publication of "The Temperance Problem and Social Reform," by Joseph Rowntree and Arthur Sherwell, in 1899, a volume which was the first to treat the subject scientifically on a large scale. I took the lead on the question, and finally two tracts were published in 1898, "Liquor Licensing at Home and Abroad" (No. 85), giving a sketch of the facts, and "Municipal Drink Traffic" (No. 86), which set out a scheme drafted by me, but substantially modified as the result of discussions by the Executive Committee and by meetings of members. This is one of the few causes taken up by the Society which has made but little progress in popular favour in the seventeen years that have elapsed since we adopted it.

Old Age Pensions, proposed in 1890 by Sidney Webb in Tract 17, "Reform of the Poor Law," was definitely advocated in Tract No. 73, "The Case for State Pensions in Old Age," written in 1896 by George Turner, one of the cleverest of the younger members. The Society did not make itself responsible for the scheme he proposed, universal pensions for all, and the Old Age Pensions Act of 1908 adopted another plan.

In 1899 and 1900 we devoted much time to the working out of further schemes of municipalisation in the form of a series of leaflets, Nos. 90 to 97. We applied the principle to Milk, Pawnshops, Slaughterhouses, Bakeries, Fire Insurance, and Steamboats. These were written by various members, and are all careful little studies of the subject, but they were not issued in a convenient form, and none of the schemes advocated has yet been generally carried out.

The Tariff Reform agitation could not pass unnoticed, and for a time Bernard Shaw showed a certain inclination to toy with it. A tract advocating Free Trade was actually set up, but got no further. Finally Shaw drafted "Fabianism and the Fiscal Question; An Alternative Policy" (Tract 116), which we adopted with practical unanimity, though it was the occasion of the resignation of Graham Wallas.

It was perhaps the least successful of the many pronouncements written by Bernard Shaw on behalf of the Society. A subtle and argumentative criticism of Mr. Chamberlain's policy on one side and of the Free Trade rejoinder on the other is neither simple nor decisive enough for the general reader: and the alternatives advocated — reorganisation of the consular service in the interests of export trade, free ocean transit for the purpose of consolidating the Empire and nationalisation of railways as a necessary corollary together with improved technical education — were too futurist, and appealed directly to too small and conservative a class, to attract much attention in the heat of a vital controversy. The writer had no anticipation of the triumph of Liberalism, then so near, and evidently expected that Mr. Chamberlain would carry the country for his policy. The tract was also issued in a shilling edition on superior paper with a preface by the author, and it is the only one of his publications which has failed to sell freely.

At this period we had a number of Committees appointed to investigate various problems, and one of them, which had for its reference the Birth-rate and Infant Mortality, produced a report of more than temporary significance. When the Society was formed the Malthusian hypothesis held the field unchallenged and the stock argument against Socialism was that it would lead to universal misery by removing the beneficent checks on the growth of population, imposed by starvation and disease upon the lowest stratum of society. Since the year 1876 the birth-rate had declined, and gradually the fear of over-population, which had saddened the lives of such men as John Stuart Mill, began to give way to the much less terrifying but still substantial fear of under-population, caused either by race degeneracy or race suicide. At that period the former of the two was the accepted explanation, and only by vague hints did scientific statisticians indicate that there might be or perhaps must be something else than "natural" causes for the decline. To the Society it seemed an all-important question. Was our race to perish by sterility, and if so, was sterility due to wealth and luxury or to poverty and disease? Or was the cause of the decline a voluntary limitation of families? We determined, as a first step, to form some sort of statistical estimate of the extent of voluntary restriction. We thought, and, as the event proved, thought rightly, that our members would be willing to assist us in this delicate enquiry. They were a sample of the population, selected in a manner which bore no sort of relation to the question at issue, and if we could get returns from them indicating their personal practice in the matter, we might have some clue to the facts. It turned out that the result was far more startling and far more conclusive than we suspected.

In November, 1905, carefully drafted enquiry forms were sent out to all members of the Society except unmarried women, so arranged as to allow exact answers to be given to the questions without disclosure of the name or handwriting of the deponent. Of the 634 posted 460 were returned or accounted for, and only two members signified objection to the enquiry. After deduction of bachelors and others not relevant, we obtained particulars of 316 marriages. I prepared an elaborate statistical report, which showed that in the period 1890-1899 out of 120 marriages only 6 fertile marriages were recorded in which no restriction had been adopted. This was the first and possibly is the only statistical enquiry yet made on the subject, and although the number of cases was minute in proportion to the population, the evidence afforded by that sample was sufficient to be conclusive, that at any rate a cause, and probably the chief cause, of the fall in the birth-rate was voluntary limitation of families.

The method of publication presented some difficulty, and finally it was decided, in order to secure the most generally impressive publicity, to ask Sidney Webb to collect the other available evidence and to make an article out of the whole, to be published over his name. It appeared as two special articles in "The Times" for October 11th and 18th, 1906, and was subsequently reprinted by us as Tract 131, "The Decline of the Birth-rate."

Other Committees at this period discussed Agriculture, Poor Law, Local Government Areas, Public Control of Electricity, and Feeding of School Children. Reports on all these subjects were issued as tracts, some of which have been mentioned already in connection with their authors, H.W. Macrosty and Hubert Bland, whilst others will be referred to in a future chapter.

Chapter IX   The Episode of Mr. Wells: 1906-8

His lecture on administrative areas – "Faults of the Fabian" – The Enquiry Committee – The Report, and the Reply – The real issue, Wells v. Shaw – The women intervene – The Basis altered – The new Executive – Mr. Wells withdraws – His work for Socialism – The writing of Fabian Tracts.

The long controversy introduced by Mr. H.G. Wells attracted much public attention to the Fabian Society, added greatly to its numbers, and for a time made it more of a popular institution than it had been before or has been since. But, in fact, its main permanent interest arises from the persons who played the leading parts. The real question at issue was one neither of Socialist theory nor of Socialist policy. In so far as these entered in, Mr. Wells preached to willing listeners, and the only difference of opinion was as to the relative stress to be laid on particular points. When the episode was over, the chief change made in Fabian policy was one which Mr. Wells did not initiate, and which as soon as it was actually adopted he virtually repudiated. The substance of the controversy was whether the members desired to hand over their Society to be managed by Mr. Wells alone, or whether they preferred to retain their old leaders and only to accept Mr. Wells as one amongst the rest.

Mr. Wells became a member in February, 1903, and in March gave his first lecture to the Society on a very technical subject, "The Question of Scientific Administrative Areas in Relation to Municipal

Undertakings," a paper subsequently published as an appendix to "Mankind in the Making."

It was probably his first appearance on a public platform; and as a lecture it was by no means a success, because he read his paper in a low monotonous voice, addressed to a corner of the hall. If Mr. Wells had been by nature or practice as effective in speaking as he is in writing the fate of the Fabian Society might have been different. He was severely handicapped in his contest with the skilled debaters of the "Old Gang," and though after a short time he learnt the art up to a point, he was never really at home on a platform, and since the Fabian episode he has confined himself for the most part to controversy in writing.

The next contribution of Mr. Wells to Fabian propaganda was on January 12th, 1906. This date had been fixed for his paper next referred to, but in view of the General Election then in progress he read in its place his admirable article entitled "This Misery of Boots," which was subsequently issued as a special Fabian publication.

On February 9th the great controversy began by the paper entitled "Faults of the Fabian," read by Mr. Wells to a members' meeting, and subsequently issued as a private document to all the members of the Society. It was couched altogether in a friendly tone, expressed cordial appreciation of the record of the Society, but criticised it for lack of imaginative megalomania. It was "still half a drawing-room society," lodged in "an underground apartment," or "cellar," with one secretary and one assistant. "The first of the faults of the Fabian, then, is that it is small, and the second that strikes me is that, even for its smallness, it is needlessly poor." The task undertaken by the Fabians "is nothing less than the alteration of the economic basis of society. Measure with your eye this little meeting, this little hall: look at that little stall of not very powerful tracts: think of the scattered members, one here, one there.... Then go out into the Strand. Note the size of the buildings and business places, note the glare of the advertisements, note the abundance of traffic and the multitude of people.... That is the world whose very foundations you are attempting to change. How does this little dribble of activities look then?"

The paper goes on to complain that the Society did not advertise itself, made the election of new members difficult, and maintained a Basis "ill-written and old-fashioned, harsh and bad in tone, assertive and unwise." The self-effacive habits and insidious methods of the

Society were next criticised, and the writer exclaimed, "Make Socialists and you will achieve Socialism; there is no other plan." The history of the Fabian motto was made use of to enforce the view that victory can only be gained by straight fighters like Scipio, whilst Fabius, however successful at first, ended his career as a stumbling-block to progress. To effect the desired expansion the writer proposed to raise an income of £1000 a year, to increase the staff, to prepare literature for the conversion of unbelievers, and to get a number of young men and women, some paid and some unpaid, to carry on the propaganda and the administrative work. "Unless I am the most unsubstantial of dreamers, such a propaganda as I am now putting before you ought to carry our numbers up towards ten thousand within a year or so of its commencement."

At the close of the meeting it was unanimously agreed "that the Executive Committee be instructed to appoint a Committee consisting of members and non-members of the Executive to consider what measures should be taken to increase the scope, influence, income, and activity of the Society." Further, a temporary amendment was made to the rules deferring the Annual Meeting and Executive election until after the Committee had reported.

"The Executive Committee," says "Fabian News," "was of opinion that a large Committee including both the Executive and an equal number of unofficial members should be appointed. But as Mr. Wells, the author of the proposal, was resolutely opposed to this plan, the Executive decided that in the circumstances it was best to fall in with his wishes, and they accordingly appointed only those members, both Executive and other, whom Mr. Wells nominated and who were willing to serve."

The Committee thus appointed consisted of the Rev. Stewart Headlam, Mrs. Bernard Shaw, and G.R.S. Taylor of the Executive; Dr. Stanton Coit, W.A. Colegate, Dr. Haden Guest, Sydney Olivier, Mrs. Pember Reeves, H.G. Wells, and Mrs. Wells.

The Committee held its first sitting on February 28th, but its report was not completed and presented to the Executive until the following October, Mr. Wells having in the interval visited the United States.

"Faults of the Fabian," written before the election of 1906, gave little indication that its author anticipated the sudden outburst of interest in Socialism which followed the astonishing success of the Labour Party at the polls. When Keir Hardie was chosen as leader of the party, it was recognised that Socialism was no longer the creed of a few fanatics, but a political force supported, actively or passively, by the great organisations of Labour throughout the country, able to fight, and sometimes to beat both the older parties. A new era in politics had begun. The Tories had been defeated before by Mr. Gladstone's unrivalled personality. Now they were defeated, as they had not been for three-quarters of a century, by a party none of whose leaders possessed an outstanding personality, and by a programme which contained no item with any popular appeal. Everybody was thinking and talking politics; every political conversation began or ended with that unknown factor, the new Labour Party; every discussion of the Labour Party involved a discussion of Socialism.

Perhaps Mr. Wells with the intuition of genius in fact foresaw what was about to happen: perhaps it was only chance. Anyway his proposal for an enlarged and invigorated society came at the precise moment, when the realisation of his project was in fact possible; and, of course, his own vigorous and interesting personality attracted many to us who might have moved in other directions, or indeed never have moved at all.

The inner history of the Wells Committee has never been revealed, but the composition of the Committee indicates the probable truth of the rumours that the meetings were anything but dull, though in the end the Committee arrived at an unanimous report. Sydney Olivier was one of the "old gang," though at that time a vigorous supporter of all sorts of changes. Mr. Headlam has always stood at the extreme right of the movement, and in party politics has never abated his loyalty to Liberalism. Mr. G.R.S. Taylor and Dr. Haden Guest were at that time eager adherents of the Labour Party, and Dr. Coit, who had just fought an election for the Party, no doubt took the same line. Mrs. Shaw by habit and Mrs. Reeves by instinct belonged to the government rather than to the opposition: and Mr. Colegate, a judicious person, then quite young, doubtless inclined to the same side. Last but not least, Mr. Wells himself, then as always mercurial in his opinions, but none the less intensely opinionated, and unable to believe that anybody could honestly differ from him, was by himself sufficient to disturb the harmony of any committee.

Mrs. Wells acted as secretary, and the Committee took evidence from myself and others before the report was drawn up.

The Report of the Committee is a much less inspiring document than the irresponsible and entertaining "Faults of the Fabian." It was largely concerned with a number of administrative details. New books and "short readable tracts" were to be written, and the format of our publications was to be changed. Groups were to be revived in all localities (to be called "Wandsworth 1, Wandsworth 2, Wandsworth 3," and so on), together with Head-quarters groups, also numbered 1, 2, 3, etc. This perhaps is the chief remaining trace of the megalomania of the original scheme, and is hidden away in an appendix: all our efforts never yielded Wandsworth No. 1, let alone the others! A fixed minimum subscription payable on a fixed date and a list of subscriptions to be published annually were further suggestions. The rule of the Society had been and is to the contrary in both particulars. "Fabian News" was to be enlarged into a weekly review addressed to the public, a change which would have required an editorial staff and extensive new offices. A publications editor was to be appointed who would be able to publish, or to arrange for the publication of, such books as Mr. Wells' "A Modern Utopia" and Mr. Money's "Riches and Poverty." The Basis of the Society was to be rewritten, its name changed to the British Socialist Party — a title since adopted by the old Social Democratic Federation — the Executive Committee was to be replaced by a Council of twenty-five, which was to appoint three Committees of three members each for Publishing, for Propaganda, and General Purposes respectively. The last, to be entitled the Directing Committee, was to meet frequently and manage most of the affairs of the Society. Finally, "in harmonious co-operation with other Socialist and Labour bodies," the Society was to run candidates for Parliament and raise a fund for the purpose.

It will be seen that some of these proposals were merely speculative. Groups could be organised easily enough when the members in any district numbered hundreds instead of units, or, at best, dozens. New tracts could be published when they were written: a weekly review was possible if the capital was provided. The new Basis and the new name were matters of emphasis and taste rather than anything else. The new machinery of government was in the main a question to be decided by experience. Mr. Wells had none; it is said that he never sat on a Committee before that under discussion, and certainly while he remained a Fabian he never acquired the Committee habit. On the principle underlying some of these proposals, viz. that the Society should cease to treat membership as a privilege, and should aim at increasing its numbers, there was no serious controversy. The Executive Committee had already carried through a suggestion made in the discussion on "Faults of the Fabian" for the creation of a class of Associates, entitled to all privileges except control over policy, with a view to provide a means of attracting new adherents. The one constructive proposal, direct collective participation in Parliamentary Elections, was quite alien to Mr. Wells' original ideas; it was forced on him, it is said, by other members of his Committee and was described by himself later on as "secondary and subordinate."

The Executive Committee transmitted the Special Committee's Report to the members of the Society accompanied by a Report of their own, drafted by Bernard Shaw and incomparably superior to the other as a piece of literature.

The reply of the Executive Committee began by welcoming criticism from within the Society, of which they complained that in the past they had had too little. An opposition, they said, was a requisite of good government. They were prepared to welcome expansion, but they pointed out that the handsome offices proposed must be produced by the large income and not the income by the handsome offices. A publishing business on the scale suggested could not be undertaken by an unincorporated society; moreover, at present the Society had not sufficient income to pay its officials at the market rate, or to keep out of debt to its printer. They agreed that the Executive Committee should be enlarged, but recommended twenty-one instead of twenty-five members; and that the three proposed sub-committees be appointed, but of seven members each instead of three. The project of triumvirates they could not endorse, both for other reasons and because all the leading members of the Society refused to serve on them, while the essence of the scheme was that the triumvirs should be the most influential members of the Society. The abolition of the old-fashioned restrictions on admission to membership was approved, but not the proposal for a fixed subscription payable on an appointed date. The Executive Committee did not object to the proposed new Basis as a whole (and in fact it is on record that its adoption by the Executive was only lost by 7 votes to 6); but considered that passages were open to criticism and that the time and effort necessary for carrying through any new Basis, so worded as to unite practically the whole Society, would be better spent in other ways. A Socialist weekly would be valuable, but it would not replace "Fabian News," which was required for the internal purposes of the Society, and capable journalists like Mr. Wells himself preferred the publicity of the "Fortnightly Review" and "The Times," to the "Clarion" and the "Labour Leader." The Reply goes at great length into the difficulty of forming a Socialist Party, and into the composition and policy of the Labour Party, all admirably argued, but just a little unreal; for Bernard Shaw has never quite understood the Labour Party which he did so much to create, and at the same time he is thoroughly convinced that he sees it as it is, in the white light of his genius. Permeation is described, explained, and defended—the Special Committee had suggested rather than proposed, in scarcely more than a sentence, that the policy be abandoned—and it is announced that as long as the Executive was unchanged there would be no reversal of the political policy of the Society. Finally the Reply asserts that the time had come to attempt the formation of a middle-class Socialist Party. At the end three resolutions were set out, which the Executive submitted to the Society for discussion.

How much of personality, how little of principle there was in the great controversy is indicated by the fact that Mrs. Bernard Shaw signed the Special Committee Report, with the reservation that she also completely agreed with the Reply. Mr. Headlam also was a party to both documents: Mr. G.R.S. Taylor, alone of the three Executive members of the Special Committee, supported the Report and dissociated himself from the Reply. Of course the Executive Committee had to decide points in their Report by a majority. That majority, in the case of the proposed revision of the Basis, was, as already mentioned, one vote only. I did not concur with the view expressed about the Labour Party, a body scarcely less easy to be understood by an outsider than the Fabian Society itself: and at that time I was the only insider on the Fabian Executive.

But the real issue was a personal one. The Executive Committee at that time consisted, in addition to the three just named, of Percy Alden (Liberal M.P. for Tottenham), Hubert Bland, Cecil E. Chesterton, Dr. F. Lawson Dodd, F.W. Galton, S.G. Hobson, H.W. Macrosty, W. Stephen Sanders, Bernard Shaw, George Standring, Sidney Webb and myself. Mr. Alden was too busy with his new parliamentary duties to take much part in the affair. All the rest, except of course Mr. Taylor, stood together on the real issue—Was the Society to be controlled by those who had made it or was it to be handed over to Mr. Wells? We knew by this time that he was a masterful person, very fond of his own way, very uncertain what that way was, and quite unaware whither it necessarily led. In any position except that of leader Mr. Wells was invaluable, as long as he kept it! As leader we felt he would be impossible, and if he had won the fight he would have justly claimed a mandate to manage the Society on the lines he had laid down. As Bernard Shaw led for the Executive, the controversy was really narrowed into Wells versus Shaw.

The Report was sent to the members with "Fabian News" for December, 1906, and it was the occasion of much excitement. The Society had grown enormously during the year. The names of no less than ninety applicants for membership are printed in that month's issue alone. In March, 1907, the membership was 1267, an increase of nearly 500 in two years.

The discussion was carried on at a series of meetings held at Essex Hall, Strand, under the chairmanship of Mr. H. Bond Holding, on December 7th and 14th, 1906, and January 11th and 18th, February 1st and March 8th, and also at the Annual Meeting for 1905-6, held on February 22nd, 1907. The series was interrupted for the London County Council Election on March 2nd, in which many of the members were concerned.

With a view to a "Second Reading" debate the executive Committee had put down a general resolution that their report be received, but Mr. Wells did not fall in with this plan, and the resolution on the motion of Bernard Shaw was adopted without discussion. On the first clause of the next resolution, instructing the Executive to submit amendments to the Rules for increasing their number to twenty-five, Mr. Wells, acting for himself, moved an amendment "approving the spirit of the report of the Committee of Enquiry, and desiring the outgoing Executive to make the earliest possible arrangements for the election of a new Executive to give effect to that report." His speech, which occupied an hour and a quarter and covered the whole field, would have been great if Mr. Wells had been a good speaker. Written out from notes, it was printed in full by himself for circulation amongst the members, and it is vigorous, picturesque entertaining, and imaginative, as his work always is. But it delivered him into the hands of his more experienced opponents by virtually challenging the society to discard them and enter on a regenerated career under his guidance. It was a heroic issue to force; and it was perhaps the real one; but it could have only one result. The discussion was adjourned to the 14th, and at 9 o'clock on that evening Bernard Shaw replied on the whole debate. His main proposition was that, as the amendment had been converted by Mr. Wells' printed and circulated speech into a motion of want of confidence, the leaders of the Society must and would retire if it were adopted. They were willing to discuss every point on its merits and to abide by the decision of the Society, but they would not accept a general approval of the Committee's Report as against their own when it implied an accusation of misconduct. In the course of the speech Mr. Wells pledged himself not to retire from the Society if he was defeated; and at the end of it he consented to withdraw his amendment. Bernard Shaw's speech, probably the most impressive he has ever made in the Society, was delivered to a large and keenly appreciative audience in a state of extreme excitement. A long report pacifically toned down by Shaw himself, appears in "Fabian News" (January, 1907). It succeeded in its object. The Executive Committee welcomed the co-operation of Mr. Wells; the last thing they desired was to drive him out of the Society, and whilst they could not accept his report as a whole, they were willing to adopt any particular item after full discussion. There is no doubt that they would have won if the amendment had gone to a division, but they were only too glad not to inflict a defeat on their opponents.

The next episode in the debate requires a few words of introduction. The Society had always been in favour of votes for women. A proposition in the Manifesto, Tract No. 2, published as early as 1884, states that "men no longer need special political privileges to protect them against women," and in all our publications relating to the franchise or local government the claims of women to equal citizenship were prominently put forward. But we had published no tract specially on the subject of the Parliamentary Vote for Women. This was not mere neglect. In 1893 a committee was appointed "to draw up a tract advocating the claims of women to all civil and political rights at present enjoyed by men," and in March, 1894, it reported that "a tract had been prepared which the Committee itself did not consider suitable for publication." Later the Committee was discharged, and in face of this fiasco nothing further was done.

Mr. Wells took a strong view on the importance of doing something in relation to women and children, though exactly what he proposed was never clear. He offered to the Society his little book on "Socialism and the Family," subsequently published by Mr. Fifield, but the Executive Committee declined it precisely because of its vagueness: they were not disposed to accept responsibility for criticisms on the existing system, unless some definite line of reform was proposed which they could ask the Society to discuss and approve, or at any rate to issue as a well-considered scheme suitable for presentation to the public.

The new Basis proposed by the Special Committee declared that the Society sought to bring about "a reconstruction of the social organisation" by

(a.) promoting transfer of land and capital to the State,

(b.) "enforcing equal citizenship of men and women,

(c.) "substituting public for private authority in the education and support of the young."

Precisely what the last clause meant has never been disclosed. Mr. Wells in his speech did nothing to elucidate it. Mr. Shaw in his reply criticised its vagueness and protested against possible interpretations of it. Mr. Wells stated some time later that he had resigned from the Society because we refused to adopt it. I do not think that any of his colleagues attached much importance to it, and none of them has attempted to raise the issue since.

Clause (b) was another matter. Nobody objected to the principle of this, but many demurred to inserting it in the Basis. We regarded the Basis as a statement of the minimum of Socialism, without which no man had the right to call himself a Socialist. But there are a few Socialists, such as Mr. Belfort Bax, who are opposed to women's suffrage, and moreover, however important it be, some of us regard it as a question of Democracy rather than Socialism. Certainly no one would contend that approval of women's suffrage was acceptance of a part of the creed of Socialism. It is a belief compatible with the most thoroughgoing individualism.

But many of the women members had made up their minds that this clause must appear in the Basis, and under the leadership of Mrs. Pember Reeves, they had indicated they would vote for the Special Committee Report unless they got their way. Those who, like myself, regarded this amendment of the Basis as inexpedient, recognised also that the adoption of the Wells report was far more inexpedient, and the Executive consequently decided to support a proposal that they be instructed to submit an addition to the Basis declaring for equal citizenship for men and women. On January 11th, 1907, Mrs. Pember Reeves obtained precedence for a resolution to this effect, and she was seconded by Mrs. Sidney Webb, who, after fourteen years of membership, was now beginning to take a part in the business of the Society. The opposition was led by Dr. Mary O'Brien Harris, who objected not to the principle but to its inclusion in the Basis, but she was unsuccessful, and the instruction was carried.

On January 18th the debate on the Executive resolutions was resumed, and it was resolved to increase the Executive Committee to twenty-one, to form three standing Sub-Committees, and to abolish the old restrictions on membership. On February 1st the debate on Political Action began, and largely turned on the question whether we should attempt to found a Socialist Party or should subordinate our political activity to the Independent Labour Party. As the first step towards founding a middle-class Socialist Party was to be the establishment of Fabian Societies throughout the country, those of us who like myself did not believe in the possibility of the proposed new party could none the less support the scheme. Co-operation with the Labour Party was not in question; nor was the continuance of our friendly relations with the I.L.P., but the proposal to subordinate our political activity to the latter society met with but little support, and finally on March 2nd the Executive resolution to appoint a Committee for the purpose of drawing up a political policy was adopted against a very small minority. Mr. Wells took very little part in the proceedings after the Second Reading debate, and only one speech of his is mentioned in the report.

Meanwhile the controversy was being fought out on another field. The January meetings had settled the number of the new Executive and decided how the Basis should be altered. The Executive therefore was now able to summon the Annual Meeting in order to make the necessary amendments to the Rules. This was held on February 22nd, when the resolutions were adopted without discussion. The meeting then took up some minor items in the Report, and in particular certain other amendments to the Basis proposed by individual members. On these a resolution was carried that the new Executive appoint a Committee to revise the Basis. The Committee was in fact appointed, and consisted of Bernard Shaw, Sidney Webb, H.G. Wells, and Sidney Ball of Oxford. Mr. Wells resigned from the Society before its labours were completed, and no report was ever presented.

The Annual Meeting over, the way was now clear for the election of the new Executive. The ballot papers, sent out with the March

"News," contained the names of 37 candidates, 13 out of the 15 of the retiring Committee and 24 others. In normal years the practice of issuing election addresses is strictly discouraged, because of the advantage they give to those rich enough to afford the expense. Therefore the record of new candidates, severely concrete statements of past achievements, is published in "Fabian News." On this occasion the usual distinction between old and new candidates was not made, and the Executive undertook to send out Election Addresses of candidates subject to necessary limits and on payment by the candidates of the cost of printing. In addition numerous other addresses were posted to the electors. The Old Gang made no attempt to monopolise the Executive by running a full ticket. The candidates in effect formed three groups, 15 supporters of the outgoing Executive, including 10 retiring members who issued a joint address; 13 candidates selected by a temporary Reform Committee whose names were sent out by Mr. Wells and his chief adherents; 7 independents, some of them supporters of the Executive and the others of the Reformers; and finally myself. As I was paid secretary and returning officer I did not formally associate myself with any party, though my general sympathy with my old colleagues was well known. Nine hundred and fifty-four members cast very nearly 17,000 votes. Sidney Webb headed the poll with 819 votes; I followed with 809. Bernard Shaw received 781, and Mr. Wells came fourth with 717. All the retiring members were re-elected except Cecil Chesterton, and including G.R.S. Taylor, who had vehemently opposed his colleagues. Eleven of the Executive list, nine of the Reformers, and myself constituted the new Committee. In fact it was an able and effective body. The Old Gang brought in Mr. Granville Barker; the Reformers included Mr. Wells, Mrs. Pember Reeves, Aylmer Maude, R.C.K. Ensor, Dr. Haden Guest, Sidney Ball, F.W. Pethick Lawrence, and Miss B.L. Hutchins—most, if not all, of whom received support from the friends of the Old Gang. Scarcely anything less like revolutionists can be imagined than this list. Mr. Pethick Lawrence, it is true, has since then done some hard fighting in another cause, but he has always acted with seriousness and deliberation. Most of the others might as well have figured on one ticket as the other. The Old Gang including myself had 12 votes and all the experience, against 9 on the other side. But the two sides did not survive the first meeting of the new Committee. There was, as I have already said, no differences of principle between the two parties. The expansion of the parent Society had come about, local Societies were growing up all over the country; Mr. Wells said no more about public authority over the young—indeed his election address made no reference to it—and Mr. Shaw did nothing to establish his Middle-Class Socialist Party.

The new Committee quickly settled down to work, but Mr. Wells was already wearying of his rôle as political organiser. He was appointed both to the General Purposes and the Propaganda Sub-Committees, but after attending two meetings of the former, and none of the latter, he resigned from both in October, and of the seventeen meetings of the Executive Committee during its year of office he attended only seven.

In April, 1908, he was re-elected to the Executive, again fourth on the poll, and Mrs. Wells who had not been a candidate before was also successful. But in the following September he resigned his membership of the Society, assigning as reasons "disagreement with the Basis which forms the Confession of Faith of the Society and discontent with the general form of its activities," together with a desire "to concentrate on the writing of novels." He explained that "a scheme which proposes to leave mother and child economically dependent on the father is not to me Socialism at all, but a miserable perversion of Socialism." The letter, printed in "Fabian News," goes on to refer to his objection to the "no compensation" clause in the Basis (the real weakness of which is that it refers hypothetically to a complete change of system and is never applied to any particular case), and added that the opportunity for a propaganda to the British middle classes was now over. Mrs. Wells retained her seat on the Executive Committee till March, 1910, and soon after that date the connection of both of them with the Society altogether ceased.

I have now traced the main stream of the subject of this chapter, though a good deal remains to be said on other effects of the agitation. I have indicated that the actual proposals made by the Special Committee under the inspiration of Mr. Wells, in so far at any rate as they were controversial or controverted, were futile or impossible, and neither led, nor in my opinion could have led, to any benefit to the Society or to its objects. But it must not be inferred from this that the intervention of Mr. Wells, viewed as a whole, was of this character. He is a man of outstanding genius, and in so far as he used his powers appropriately, his work was of enormous value to Socialism; and his energy and attractive personality added radiance to the Society only equalled in the early days when the seven Essayists were all in the field and all fighting at their bravest. The new life in the Society during those brilliant years was due to other factors as well as Mr. Wells. Other Socialist Societies, in which he took no part, also increased their numbers and launched out into fresh activities. But for us Mr. Wells was the spur which goaded us on, and though at the time we were often forced to resent his want of tact, his difficult public manners, and his constant shiftings of policy, we recognised then, and we remember still, how much of permanent value he achieved.

Of this the chiefest is his books, and as the Society as such had no part in them, anything more than a reference to them is outside the scope of this volume. But it must be said that his "New Worlds for Old," published in 1908, whilst he was a member of the Fabian Executive, is perhaps the best recent book on English Socialism.

In this connection Mr. Wells displayed unexpected modesty and at the same time inexperience of the ways of the world. His first criticism of the Society, his first project of reform, related to our tracts. To this point he directed an unpublished preface to his paper "This Misery of Boots," when he read it to the Society before the controversy had actually started. He justly observed that very few of our publications were addressed to the unconverted, were emotional appeals to join our movement, or effective explanations of our general principles. He said that these ought to be written, and the odd thing is that he appeared to imagine that anybody, or at any rate a considerable number of people, could just sit down and write them. He was aware that he could do it himself, and he innocently imagined that plenty of other people could do it too. He blamed the Executive for failing to make use of the members in this respect, and persuaded them to invite any member to send in manuscripts.

In fact of course something like genius, or, at any rate, very rare ability, is required for this sort of work. Any competent writer can collect the facts about Municipal Drink Trade, or Afforestation, or Poor Law Reform: many can explain an Act of Parliament in simple language: but only one here and there can write what others care to read on the principles of Socialism and the broad aspects of its propaganda. If our list of tracts be examined it will be found that the great majority of the "general" tracts have been written by Sidney Webb and Bernard Shaw. A few other writers have contributed general tracts from a special standpoint, such as those on Christian

Socialism. When we have mentioned reprinted papers by William Morris and Sir Oliver Lodge, and a tract by Sidney Ball, the list is virtually complete. Mr. Wells himself only contributed to us his paper "This Misery of Boots," and his appeal to the rank and file yielded nothing at all. Of course there are plenty of people as innocent in this respect as Mr. Wells was at that period referred to. Hardly a month has passed in the last twenty years without somebody, usually from the remote provinces, sending up a paper on Socialism, which he is willing to allow the Society to publish on reasonable terms. But only once have we thus found an unknown author whose work, on a special subject, we could publish, and he resigned a year or two later because we were compelled to reject a second tract which he wrote for us.

The history of the intervention of Mr. Wells is now complete. Some account of the expansion of the Society at this period will be given in the next chapter.

Chapter X   The Policy of Expansion: 1907-12

Statistics of growth – The psychology of the Recruit – Famous Fabians – The Arts Group – The Nursery – The Women's Group – Provincial Fabian Societies – University Fabian Societies – London Groups revived – Annual Conferences – The Summer School – The story of "Socialist Unity" – The Local Government Information Bureau – The Joint Standing Committee – Intervention of the International Socialist Bureau.

The episode described in the last chapter, which took place during the years 1906 to 1908, was accompanied by many other developments in the activities of the Society which must now be described. In the first place the membership grew at an unprecedented rate. In the year ended March, 1905, 67 members were elected. Next year the number was 167, to March, 1907, it was 455, to March, 1908, 817, and to March, 1909, 665. This was an enormous accession of new blood to a society which in 1904 had only 730 members in all. In 1909 the Society consisted of 1674 men and 788 women, a total of 2462; of these 1277 were ordinary members residing in or near London, 343 scattered elsewhere in the United Kingdom, 89 abroad; 414 were members of provincial Societies and 339 of University Societies. There were in addition about 500 members of local Fabian Societies who were not also members of the London Society, and the Associates numbered 217. The income from subscriptions of all sorts was £473 in 1904 and

£1608 in 1908, the high-water mark in the history of the Society for contributions to the ordinary funds.

Of course there is all the difference in the world between a new member and an old. The freshly elected candidate attends every meeting and reads every word of "Fabian News." He begins, naturally, as a whole-hearted admirer and is profoundly impressed with the brilliance of the speakers, the efficiency of the organisation, the ability of the tracts. A year or two later, if he has any restlessness of intellect, he usually becomes a critic: he wants to know why there are not more brightly written tracts, explanatory of Socialism and suitable for the unconverted: he complains that the lectures are far less interesting than they used to be, that the debates are footling, the publications unattractive in appearance and too dull to read. A few years later he either settles down into a steady-going member, satisfied to do what little he can to improve this unsatisfactory world; or else, like Mr. Wells, he announces that the Society is no longer any good: once (when he joined) it was really important and effective: its methods *were* all right: it *was* proclaiming a fresh political gospel. But times have changed, whilst the Society has only grown old: it has done its work, and missed its opportunity for more. It is no longer worthy of his support.

In 1907 and 1908 the Society consisted largely of new members; consequently the meetings were crowded and we were driven out from one hall after another. Moreover the propagandist enthusiasm of Mr. Wells and the glamour of his name helped to attract a large number of distinguished persons into our ranks. Mr. Granville Barker was one of the most active of these. He served on the Executive from 1907 to 1912 and took a large share in the detailed work of the Committees, besides giving many lectures and assisting in social functions. The Rev. R.J. Campbell, who addressed large meetings on several occasions, was also elected to the Executive for the year 1908-9, but did not attend a single meeting. Mr. Aylmer Maude joined the Executive in 1907, held office to 1912, and is still a working member of the Society. Arnold Bennett, Laurence Irving, Edgar Jepson, Reginald Bray, L.C.C. (member of the Executive 1911-12), Sir Leo (then Mr.) Chiozza Money, M.P. (who sat on the Executive from 1908 to 1911), Dr. Stanton Coit, H. Hamilton Fyfe, A.R. Orage, G.M. Trevelyan, Edward Garnett, Dr. G.B. Clark (for many years M.P.), Miss Constance Smedley, Philip Snowden, M.P., Mrs. Snowden (Executive 1908-9), George Lansbury, Herbert Trench, Jerome K. Jerome, Edwin

Pugh, Spencer Pryse, and A. Clutton Brock are amongst the people known in politics, literature, or the arts who joined the Society about this period.

Some of these took little or no part in our proceedings, beyond paying the necessary subscription, but others lectured or wrote for the Society or participated in discussions and social meetings. These were at this time immensely successful. In the autumn of 1907, for example, Mrs. Bernard Shaw arranged for the Society a series of crowded meetings of members and subscribers at Essex Hall on "The Faith I Hold." Mrs. Sidney Webb led off and was followed by the Rev. R.J. Campbell, S.G. Hobson, Dr. Stanton Coit, H.G. Wells, and Hubert Bland: with an additional discourse later in the spring by Sir Sydney Olivier. Mr. Wells' paper, which proved to be far too long for a lecture, was the first draft of his book "First and Last Things"; but he had tired of the Society when it was published, and the preface conceals its origin in something of a mystery. Sir John Gorst, Mrs. Annie Besant, Dr. Südekum (German M.P.), Sir John Cockburn, K.C.M.G., the Hon. W.P. Reeves, Raymond Unwin, and Sir Leo Chiozza Money were amongst the other lecturers of that year.

In 1906 and succeeding years a new form of organisation was established. Members spontaneously associated themselves into groups, "The Nursery" for the young, the Women's Group, the Arts Group, and Groups for Education, Biology, and Local Government. The careers of these bodies were various. The Arts Group included philosophy, and, to tell the truth, almost excluded Socialism. But all of us in our youth are anxiously concerned about philosophy and art and many who are no longer young are in the same case. Moreover artists and philosophers are always attractive. Mr. Holbrook Jackson and Mr. A.R. Orage, at that time associated in "The New Age," founded the group early in 1907, and soon obtained lecturers as distinguished, and audiences scarcely less numerous than the Society itself. But in eighteen months "Art and Philosophy in Relation to Socialism" seems to have been exhausted, and after the summer of 1908 the Group disappears from the calendar. Biology and Local Government had a somewhat longer but far less glorious career. The meetings were small and more of the nature of classes. Education is the life-work of a large class, which provides a sensible proportion of Fabian membership, and teachers are always eager to discuss and explain the difficult problems of their profession and the complex law which regulates it. The Education Group has led a diligent and useful life; it prepared a tract (No. 156), "What an Education Committee can do (Elementary Schools)," and besides its private meetings it arranges occasional lectures open to the public, which sometimes attract large audiences.

The Nursery belongs to another class. When a society, formed as many societies are, of quite young people, has existed over twenty years, the second generation begins to be adult, and wants to be quit of its parents. Moreover the young desire, naturally, to hear themselves talk, whilst the others usually prefer the older and more famous personages. So a number of younger members eagerly took up a plan which originated in the circle of the Bland family, for forming a group confined to the young in years or in membership in order to escape the overmastering presence of the elderly and experienced. Sometimes they invite a senior to talk to them and to be heckled at leisure. More often they provide their own fare from amongst themselves. Naturally the Nursery is not exclusively devoted to economics and politics: picnics and dances also have their place. Some of the members eventually marry each other, and there is no better security for prolonged happiness in marriage than sympathy in regard to the larger issues of life. The Nursery has produced one tract, No. 132, "A Guide to Books for Socialists," described in the "Wells Report" as intended "to supplement or even replace that arid and indiscriminating catalogue, What to Read."

Last in date, but by no means least in importance of the Groups of this period, was the Women's Group, founded by Mrs. C.M. Wilson, who after nearly twenty years of nominal membership had resumed her active interest in the Society. The vigorous part taken by the women of the Society under the leadership of Mrs. Reeves in obtaining the only alteration yet made in the Basis has been already described. The Group was not formed till a year later, and at that time the Women's Suffrage movement, and especially the party led by Mrs. Pankhurst, had attracted universal attention. The early Suffrage movement was mainly Socialist in origin: most of the first leaders of the Women's Social and Political Union were or had been members either of the Fabian Society or of the I.L.P. and it may almost be said that all the women of the Society joined one or more of the Suffrage Societies which for the next seven years played so large a part in national politics. But besides the question of the vote, which is not peculiar to Socialism, there is a very large group of subjects of special interest to Socialist women, either practical problems of immediate politics relating to the wages and conditions of women's labour and the treatment of women by Education Acts, National Insurance Acts, and Factory Acts; or remoter and more theoretical problems, especially those connected with the question whether the wife in the ideal state is to be an independent wage-earner or the mistress and manager of an isolated home, dependent on her husband as breadwinner. Efficiently organised by Mrs. C.M. Wilson, until ill-health required her resignation of the secretaryship in 1914; by Mrs. Bernard Shaw, Mrs. Pember Reeves, Miss Murby, Miss Emma Brooke, and many others, including in later years Dr. Letitia Fairfield, the Group has had many of the characteristics of an independent society. It has its own office, latterly at 25 Tothill Street, rented from the parent Society, with its own paid assistant secretary, and it has issued for private circulation its own publications. In 1913 it prepared a volume of essays on "Women Workers in Seven Professions," which was edited by Professor Edith Morley and published by George Routledge and Sons. It has prepared five tracts for the Society, published in the general list, under a sub-title, "The Women's Group Series," and it has taken an active part, both independently and in co-operation with other bodies, in the political movements specially affecting women, which have been so numerous in recent years.

It will be recollected that the only direct result of the Special Enquiry Committee, apart from the changes made in the organisation of the Society itself, was the decision to promote local Socialist Societies of the Fabian type with a view to increasing Socialist representation in Parliament. I have recounted in a previous chapter how this scheme worked out in relation to the Labour Party and the running of candidates for Parliament. It remains to describe here its measure of success in the formation of local societies.

The summer of 1905 was about the low-water mark of provincial Fabianism. Nine societies are named in the report, but four of these appeared to have no more than a nominal existence. The Oxford University Society had but 6 members; Glasgow had 30 in its University Society and 50 in its town Society; Liverpool was reduced to 63, Leeds and County to 15, and that was all. A year later the Cambridge University Society had been formed, Oxford had more than doubled its membership to 13, but only five other societies were in existence. By the following year a revival had set in. W. Stephen Sanders, at that time an Alderman of the London County Council, who had been a member of the Society since 1890 and of the executive Committee since 1904, was appointed Organising Secretary with the special object of building up the provincial organisation. By 1910 there were forty-six local societies, and in 1912 the maximum of fifty was reached. Since then the number has declined. These societies were scattered over the country, some of them in the great cities, Manchester, Newcastle, Sheffield, and so on: others within hail of London, at Croydon, Letchworth, Ilford: others again in small towns, Canterbury, Chelmsford, Carnarvon: another was at Bedales School, Petersfield, run by my son and his schoolfellows. The local societies formed at this period, apart from the University Societies, were in the main pallid reflections of the parent Society in its earlier days; none of them had the good fortune to find a member, so far as we yet know, of even second-class rank as a thinker or speaker. One or two produced praiseworthy local tracts on housing conditions and similar subjects. They usually displayed less tolerance than the London Society, a greater inclination to insist that there was but one way of political salvation, usually the Labour Party way, and that all who would not walk in it should be treated as alien enemies. If Socialism is only to be achieved by the making of Socialists, as Mr. Wells announced with all the emphasis of a rediscovery, no doubt the local societies achieved some Socialism, since they made some members. If Socialism is to be attained by the making of Socialist measures, doubtless they accomplished a little by their influence on local administration. Organisation for political work is always educative to those who take part in it, and it has some effect on the infinitely complex parallelogram of forces which determines the direction of progress. Possibly I underestimate the importance of local Fabian Societies; there is a school of thought, often represented in the Society, which regards the provinces with reverent awe — omne ignotum pro magnifico — as the true source of political wisdom, which Londoners should endeavour to discover and obey. Londoners no doubt see little of organised labour, and even less of industrial co-operation: the agricultural labourer is to them almost a foreigner: the Welsh miner belongs to another race. But the business men, the professional class, and the political organisers of Manchester and Glasgow have, in my opinion, no better intuitions, and usually less knowledge than their equivalents in London, and they have the disadvantage of comparative isolation. London, the brain of the Empire, where reside the leaders in politics and in commerce, in literature, in journalism and in art, and which consequently attracts the young men who aspire to be the next generation of leaders, where too are stationed all the higher ranks of Civil Service, is different in kind, as well as in size, from other cities. New thought on social subjects is almost always the product of association. Only those who live in a crowd of other thinkers know where there is room for new ideas; for it takes years for the top layer of political thought to find expression in books. Therefore the provincial thinker on social problems is always a little out of date. Except for one or two University men (e.g. Sidney Ball and Sir Oliver Lodge) practically all Fabian tract-writers have been Londoners. The local Fabian Societies have so far achieved nothing towards the making of a middle-class Socialist party, and they have achieved but little else. They have been fully justified because every association for mutual instruction adds something to the mass of political intelligence, does something to disseminate ideas, but that is all that can be said for them.

The University Societies belong to a different type. Nothing is more important than the education of young men and women in politics, and the older Universities have always recognised this. Socialist Societies accordingly grew up naturally alongside Liberal and Tory Clubs, and under the shadow of the "Unions." Oxford, as we have seen, had a University Fabian Society from early days. Cambridge followed at a much later date. For years Glasgow University and University College, Aberystwyth, maintained flourishing societies. The newer Universities, dependent largely on the bounty of wealthy capitalist founders and supporters, and assisted by, or in close touch with, town councils and local industries, have been much less willing to sanction political free-thought amongst their undergraduates, and the pernicious influence of wealth, or rather the fear of alarming the wealthy, has at times induced the authorities to interfere with the freedom of the undergraduates to combine for the study and propaganda of Socialism.

Undergraduate societies are composed of a constantly shifting population, and we arranged from the first that all their members should also be elected direct to the parent Society in order that they might remain automatically in membership when they "go down." In fact of course the percentage which retains its membership is very small. "Men" and women at Universities join any organisation whose leaders at the moment are influential and popular. They are sampling life to discover what suits them, and a few years later some of them are scattered over the globe, others immersed in science or art, or wholly occupied in law and medicine, in the church and the army, in the civil service and in journalism. Most of them no doubt have ceased to pretend to take interest in social and political reform. A few remain, and these are amongst the most valuable of our members. At times, when an undergraduate of force of character and high social position, the heir to a peerage for example, is for the moment an ardent Socialist, the Fabian Society becomes, in a certain set or college, the fashionable organisation. On the whole it is true that Socialists are born and not made, and very few of the hundreds who join at such periods stay for more than a couple of years. The maximum University membership — on paper — was in 1914, when it reached 541 members, of whom 101 were at Oxford and 70 at Cambridge. But the weakness of undergraduate Socialism is indicated by the extraordinary difficulty found in paying to the parent Society the very moderate fee of a shilling a head per annum, and the effect of attempting to enforce this in 1915, combined with the propaganda of Guild Socialism, especially at Oxford, was for the moment to break up the apparently imposing array of University Fabianism.

In 1912 Clifford Allen of Cambridge formed the University Socialist Federation, which was in fact a Federation of Fabian Societies though not nominally confined to them. Mr. Allen, an eloquent speaker and admirable organiser, with most of the virtues and some of the defects of the successful propagandist, planned the foundations of the Federation on broad lines. It started a sumptuous quarterly, "The University Socialist," the contents of which by no means equalled the excellence of the print and paper. It did not survive the second number. The Federation has held several conferences, mostly at Barrow House — of which later — and issued various documents. Its object is to encourage University Socialism and to found organisations in every University. It still exists, but whether it will survive the period of depression which has coincided with the war remains to be seen.

Lastly, amongst the organs of Fabian activity come the London Groups. In the years of rapid growth that followed the publication of "Fabian Essays" the London Groups maintained a fairly genuine existence. London was teeming with political lectures, and in the decade 1889-1899 its Government was revolutionised by the County Councils Act of 1888, the Local Government Act of 1894, and the London Government Act of 1899 which established the Metropolitan Boroughs. Socialism, too, was a novelty, and the few who knew about it were in request.

Anyway even with the small membership of those days, the London Groups managed to persist, and "Fabian News" is full of reports of conferences of Group Secretaries and accounts of Group activities. In the trough of depression between the South African War and the Liberal victory of 1906 all this disappeared and the Group system scarcely existed even on paper.

With the expansion which began in 1906 the Groups revived. New members were hungry for lectures: many of them desired more opportunities to talk than the Society meetings afforded. All believed in or hoped for Mr. Wells' myriad membership. He himself was glad to address drawing-room meetings, and the other leaders did the same. Moreover the Society was conducting a series of "Suburban Lectures" by paid lecturers, in more or less middle-class residential areas of the Home Counties. Lectures to the Leisured Classes, a polite term for the idle rich, were arranged with considerable success in the West End, and other lectures, meetings, and social gatherings were incessant.

For co-ordinating these various bodies the Fabian Society has created its own form of organisation fitted to its peculiar circumstances, and more like that of the British Empire than anything else known to me. As is the United Kingdom in the British Empire, so in the Fabian movement the parent Society is larger, richer, and more powerful, and in all respects more important than all the others put together. Any form of federal organisation is impossible, because federation assumes some approach to equality amongst constituents. Our local societies, like the British self-governing Dominions, are practically independent, especially in the very important department of finance. The Groups, on the other hand, are like County Councils, local organisations within special areas for particular purposes, with their own finances for those purposes only. But the parent Society is not made up of Groups, any more than the British Government is composed of County Councils. The local Groups consist of members of the Society qualified for the group by residence in the group area; the "Subject Groups" of those associated for some particular purpose.

The problem of the Society (as it is of the Empire) was to give the local societies and the groups some real function which should emphasise and sustain the solidarity of the whole; and at the same time leave unimpaired the control of the parent Society over its own affairs.

The Second Annual Conference of Fabian Societies and Groups was held on July 6th, 1907, under the chairmanship of Hubert Bland, who opened the proceedings with an account of the first Conference held in 1892 and described in an earlier chapter. Fifteen delegates from 9 local and University Societies, 16 from 8 London Groups, 8 from Subject Groups, and 9 members of the Executive Committee were present. The business consisted of the sanction of rules for the Pan-Fabian Organisation.

The Conference of 1908 was a much bigger affair. A dozen members of the Executive, including Mr. H.G. Wells and (as he then was) Mr. L.G. Chiozza Money, M.P., and 61 delegates representing 36 Groups and Societies met for a whole-day conference at University Hall, Gordon Square. Miss Murby was chairman, and addressed the delegates on the importance of tolerance, an apposite subject in view of the discussion to follow on the proposed parliamentary action, especially the delicate issue between co-operation with the Labour Party and the promotion of a purely Socialist party. A resolution favouring exclusive support of independent Socialist candidatures moved by Mr. J.A. Allan of Glasgow received only 10 votes, but another advocating preference for such candidates was only defeated by 26 to 21. The resolution adopted left the question to be settled in each case by the constituency concerned. Another resolution directed towards condemnation of members who worked with the Liberal or Tory Party failed by 3 votes only, 17 to 20. In the afternoon Mr. Money gave an address on the Sources of Socialist Revenue, and a number of administrative matters were discussed.

The 1909 Conference was attended by 29 delegates of local and University Societies, and by 46 delegates from London Groups and from the parent Society. On this occasion a Constitution was adopted giving the Conference a regular status, the chief provisions of which required the submission to the Conference of any alteration of the Basis, and "any union affiliation or formal alliance with any other society or with any political party whereby the freedom of action of any society ... is in any way limited ... "; and of any change in the constitution itself. These are all matters which concern the local organisations, as they are required to adopt the Basis, or some approved equivalent, and are affiliated to the Labour Party through the parent Society. No contentious topic was on this occasion seriously discussed.

The Conference of 1910 was smaller, sixty-one delegates in all. Resolutions against promoting parliamentary candidatures and favouring the by this time vanishing project for an independent Socialist party obtained but little support, and the chief controversy was over an abstract resolution on the "economic independence of women," which was in the end settled by a compromise drafted by Sidney Webb.

Sixty delegates were present at the 1911 Conference, held at Clifford's Inn, who, after rejecting by a seven to one majority a resolution to confine Fabian membership to Labour Party adherents, devoted themselves mainly to opposition to the National Insurance Bill then before Parliament.

In 1912 the Conference was still large and still concerned in the position of the Society in relation to Labour and Liberalism.

Both in 1913 and in 1914 the Conference was well attended and prolonged, but in 1915, partly on account of the war and partly because of the defection of several University Societies, few were present, and the business done was inconsiderable.

The Summer School was another enterprise started at the period. It was begun independently of the Society in this sense, that half a dozen members agreed to put up the necessary capital and to accept the financial responsibility, leaving to the Society the arrangement of lectures and the management of business.

It was opened at the end of July, 1907, at Pen-yr-allt, a large house, previously used as a school, looking out over the sea, near Llanbedr, a little village on the Welsh coast between Barmouth and Harlech. The house was taken for three years partly furnished, and the committee provided the beds, cutlery, etc., needed. One or two other houses near by were usually rented for the summer months.

The value of the plan for a propagandist society is largely this, that experience shows that people can only work together efficiently when they know each other. Therefore in practice political and many other organisations find it necessary to arrange garden parties, fêtes, picnics, teas, and functions of all sorts in order to bring together their numbers under such conditions as enable them to become personally acquainted with each other. In times of expansion the Fabian Society has held dinners and soirées in London, many of which have been successful and even brilliant occasions, because the new members come in crowds and the old attend as a duty. When new members are few these entertainments cease, for nothing is so dreary as a social function that is half failure, and a hint of it brings the series to an end. But a Summer School where members pass weeks together is far more valuable in enabling the leaders and officials to find out who there is who is good as a speaker or thinker, or who is a specialist on some subject of value to the movement. Moreover, gatherings of this class attract those on the fringe of the movement, and many of our members have come to us through attendance at the school. Apart from the direct interests of the Society, a School of this character is valued by many solitary people, solitary both socially, such as teachers and civil servants, who are often lonely in the world, and solitary intellectually because they live in remote places where people of their way of thinking are scarce.

It is not necessary to describe the arrangements of the School, for these institutions have in the last few years become familiar to everybody. We do not, however, as a rule make quite such a business of the schooling as is usual where the term is short, and study is the sole object. One regular lecture a day for four days a week is the rule, but impromptu lectures or debates in the evenings, got up amongst the guests, are customary. Moreover, frequent conferences on special subjects are held, either by allied bodies, such as the Committee for the Prevention of Destitution, or by a Group, such as the Education Group or the Research Department. On these occasions the proportion of work to play is higher. The School-house belongs to the Society for the whole year, and parties are arranged for Christmas, Easter, and Whitsuntide whenever possible.

After four years at Llanbedr the lease was terminated and the original Committee wound up. The capital borrowed had all been repaid, and there remained, after a sale by auction, a lot of property and nearly £100 in cash. This the Committee transferred to the Society, and thereupon the quasi-independence of the Summer School came to an end. In 1911 a new experiment was tried. A small hotel at Saas Grund, off the Rhone Valley, was secured, and during six weeks three large parties of Fabians occupied it for periods of a fortnight each. The summer was one of the finest of recent years, and the high mountains were exceptionally attractive. On account of the remoteness of the place, and the desire to make the most of a short time, lectures were as a rule confined to the evening, and distinguished visitors were few, but an address by Dr. Hertz of Paris, one of the few French Fabians, may be mentioned, partly because in the summer of 1915 his promising career was cut short in the trenches which protected his country from the German invaders.

In 1912 Barrow House, Derwentwater, was taken for three years, a beautiful place with the Barrow Falls in the garden on one side, and grounds sloping down to the lake on the other, with its own boating pier and bathing-place. A camp of tents for men was set up, and as many as fifty or sixty guests could be accommodated at a time. Much of the success of the School has throughout been due to Miss Mary Hankinson, who from nearly the beginning has been a most popular and efficient manager. A director is selected by the Committee to act as nominal head, and holds office usually for a week or a fortnight; but the chief of staff is a permanent institution, and is not only business manager, but also organiser and leader of excursions and a principal figure in all social undertakings. A great part in arranging for the School from the first has been taken by Dr. Lawson Dodd, to whose experience and energy much of its success has been due.

The year 1911 saw the formation of the Joint Standing Committee with the I.L.P., and this is a convenient place to describe the series of attempts at Socialist Unity which began a long way back in the history of the Society. For the first eight years or so of the Socialist movement the problem of unity did not arise. Until the publication of "Fabian Essays" the Fabian Society was small, and the S.D.F., firm in its Marxian faith, and confident that the only way of salvation was its particular way, had no more idea of uniting with the other societies than the Roman Catholic Church has of union with Lutherans or Methodists. The Socialist League was the outcome of an internal dispute, and, if my memory is correct, the S.D.F. expected, not without reason, that the seceders would ultimately return to the fold. The League ceased to count when at the end of 1890 William Morris left it and reconstituted as the Hammersmith Socialist Society the branch which met in the little hall constructed out of the stable attached to Kelmscott House.

In January, 1893, seven delegates from this Society held a conference with Fabian delegates, and at a second meeting at which S.D.F. delegates were present a scheme for promoting unity was approved. A Joint Committee of five from each body assembled on February 23rd, when William Morris was appointed Chairman, with Sydney Olivier as Treasurer, and it was decided that the Chairman with H.M. Hyndman and Bernard Shaw should draft a Joint Manifesto. The "Manifesto of English Socialists," published on May 1st, 1893, as a penny pamphlet with the customary red cover, was signed by the three Secretaries, H.W. Lee of the S.D.F., Emery Walker of the H.S.S., and myself, and by fifteen delegates, including Sydney Olivier and Sidney Webb of the F.S., Harry Quelch of the S.D.F., and the three authors.

Like most joint productions of clever men, it is by no means an inspiring document. The less said, the less to dispute about, and so it only runs to eight pages of large print, four devoted to the evils of capitalism, unemployment, the decline of agriculture, and the ill-nurture of children, and the rest to remedies, a queer list, consisting of:

An eight hours law.

Prohibition of child labour for wages.

Free Maintenance for all necessitous children (a compromise in which Fabian influence may be traced by the insertion of the word "necessitous").

Equal payment of men and women for equal work.

(A principle which, whether good or bad, belongs rather to individualism than to Socialism: Socialism according to Bernard Shaw — and most of us agree with him — demands as an ideal equal maintenance irrespective of work; and in the meantime payment according to need, each to receive that share of the national product which he requires in order to do his work and maintain his dependents, if any, appropriately.)

To resume the programme:

An adequate minimum wage for all adults employed in Government and Municipal services or in any monopolies such as railways enjoying State privileges.

Suppression of all sub-contracting and sweating (an ignorant confusion between a harmless industrial method and its occasional abuse).

Universal suffrage for all adults, men and women alike.

Public payment for all public service.

These of course were only means tending towards the ideal, "to wit, the supplanting of the present state by a society of equality of condition," and then follows a sentence paraphrased from the Fabian Basis embodying a last trace of that Utopian idealism which imagines that society can be constituted so as to enable men to live in freedom without eternal vigilance, namely, "When this great change is completely carried out, the genuine liberty of all will be secured by the free play of social forces with much less coercive interference than the present system entails."

From these extracts it will be seen that the Manifesto, drafted by William Morris, but mutilated and patched up by the other two, bears the imprint neither of his style, nor that of Shaw, but reminds one rather of mid-Victorian dining-room furniture, solid, respectable, heavily ornate, and quite uninteresting. Happily there is not much of it!

Unity was attained by the total avoidance of the contentious question of political policy. But fifteen active Socialists sitting together at a period when parties were so evenly divided that a General Election was always imminent could not refrain from immediate politics, and the S.D.F., like many other bodies, always cherished the illusion that the defeat of a minority at a joint conference on a question of principle would put that minority out of action.

Accordingly, as soon as the Manifesto had been published resolutions were tabled pledging the constituent societies to concentrate their efforts on Socialist candidates accepted as suitable by the Joint Committee. On this point the Fabian Society was in a hopeless minority, and an endless vista of futile and acrimonious discussions was opened out which would lead to unrest in our own society — for there has always been a minority opposed to its dominant policy — and a waste of time and temper to the delegates from our Executive. It was therefore resolved at the end of July that our delegates be withdrawn, and that put an end to the Joint Committee.

The decision was challenged at a members' meeting by E.E. Williams, one of the signatories of the Joint Manifesto, subsequently well known as the author of "Made in Germany," and in some sense the real founder of the Tariff Reform movement; but the members by a decisive vote upheld the action of their Executive.

Four years later, early in 1897, another effort after Unity was made. By this time Morris, whose outstanding personality had given him a commanding and in some respects a moderating influence in the movement, was dead; and the Hammersmith Socialist Society had disappeared. Instead there was the new and vigorous Independent Labour Party, already the premier Socialist body in point of public influence. This body took the first step, and a meeting was held in April at the Fabian office, attended by Hubert Bland, Bernard Shaw, and myself as delegates from our Society. The proposal before the Conference was "the formation of a court of appeal to adjudicate between rival Socialist candidates standing for the same seat at any contested election," an occurrence which has in fact been rare in local and virtually unknown in Parliamentary elections.

As the Fabian Society did not at that time officially run candidates, and has always allowed to its members liberty of action in party politics, it was impossible for us to undertake that our members would obey any such tribunal. The difficulty was however solved by the S.D.F., whose delegates to the second meeting, held in July, announced that they were instructed to withdraw from the Committee if the Fabian delegates remained. The I.L.P. naturally preferred the S.D.F. to ourselves, because their actual rivalry was always with that body, and we were only too glad to accept from others the dismissal which we desired. So our delegates walked out, leaving the other two parties in temporary possession of our office, and Socialist Unity so far as we were concerned again vanished. I do not think that the court of appeal was ever constituted, and certainly the relations between the other two Societies continued to be difficult.

The next move was one of a practical character. The Fabian Society had always taken special interest in Local Government, as a method of obtaining piecemeal Socialism, and had long acted as an informal Information Bureau on the law and practice of local government administration. The success of the I.L.P. in getting its members elected to local authorities suggested a conference of such persons, which was held at Easter, 1899, on the days preceding the I.L.P. Annual Conference at Leeds. Sidney Webb was invited to be President, and gave an address on "The Sphere of Municipal Statesmanship"; Will Crooks was Chairman of the Poor Law Section. At this Conference it was resolved to form a Local Government Information Bureau, to be jointly managed by the I.L.P. and the Fabian Society; it was intended for Labour members of local authorities, but anybody could join on payment of the annual subscription of 2s. 6d. For this sum the subscriber obtained the right to have questions answered free of charge, and to receive both "Fabian News" and the official publications of the I.L.P., other than their weekly newspaper. The Bureau also published annual Reports, at first on Bills before Parliament, and latterly abstracts of such Acts passed by Parliament as were of interest to its members. It pursued an uneventful but useful career, managed virtually by the secretaries of the two societies, which divided the funds annually in proportion to the literature supplied. Several Easter Conferences of Elected Persons were held with varying success. Later on the nominal control was handed over to the Joint Committee, next to be described.

The problem of Socialist Unity seemed to be approaching a settlement when the three organisations, in 1900, joined hands with the Trade Unions in the formation of the Labour Representation Committee, later renamed the Labour Party. But in 1901, eighteen months after the Committee was constituted, the S.D.F. withdrew, and thereafter unity became more difficult than ever, since two societies were united for collective political action with the numerically and financially powerful trade unions, whilst the third took up the position of hostile isolation. But between the Fabian Society and the I.L.P. friendly relations became closer than ever. The divergent political policies of the two, the only matter over which they had differed, had been largely settled by change of circumstances. The Fabian Society had rightly held that the plan of building up an effective political party out of individual adherents to any one society was impracticable, and the I.L.P. had in fact adopted another method, the permeation of existing organisations, the Trade Unions. On the other hand the Fabian Society, which at first confined its permeation almost entirely to the Liberal Party, because this was the only existing organisation accessible — we could not work through the Trade Unions, because we were not eligible to join them — was perfectly willing to place its views before the Labour Party, from which it was assured of sympathetic attention. Neither the Fabian Society nor the I.L.P. desired to lose its identity, or to abandon its special methods. But half or two-thirds of the Fabians belonged also to the I.L.P., and nearly all the I.L.P. leaders were or had been members of the Fabian Society.

The suggestion was made in March, 1911, by Henry H. Slesser, then one of the younger members of the Executive, that the friendly relations of the two bodies should be further cemented by the formation of a Joint Standing Committee. Four members of each Executive together with the secretaries were appointed, and W.C. Anderson, later M.P. for the Attercliffe Division of Sheffield, and at that time Chairman of the I.L.P., was elected Chairman, a post which he has ever since retained. The Joint Committee has wisely confined its activities to matters about which there was no disagreement, and its proceedings have always been harmonious to the verge of dullness. The Committee began by arranging a short series of lectures, replacing for the time the ordinary Fabian meetings, and it proposed to the Labour Party a demonstration in favour of Adult Suffrage, which was successfully held at the Royal Albert Hall.

In the winter of 1912-13 the Joint Committee co-operated with the National Committee for the Prevention of Destitution (of which later) in a big War against Poverty Campaign, to demand a minimum standard of civilised life for all. A demonstration at the Albert Hall, a Conference at the Memorial Hall, twenty-nine other Conferences throughout Great Britain, all attended by numerous delegates from Trade Unions and other organisations, and innumerable separate meetings were among the activities of the Committee. In 1913 a large number of educational classes were arranged. In the winter of 1913-14 the I.L.P. desired to concentrate its attention on its own "Coming of Age Campaign," an internal affair, in which co-operation with another body was inappropriate. A few months later the War began and, for reasons explained later, joint action remains for the time in abeyance.

It will be convenient to complete the history of the movements for Socialist Unity, though it extends beyond the period assigned to this chapter, and we must now turn back to the beginning of another line of action.

The International Socialist and Trade Union Congresses held at intervals of three or four years since 1889 were at first no more than isolated Congresses, arranged by local organisations constituted for the purpose in the preceding year. Each nation voted as one, or at most, as two units, and therefore no limit was placed on the number of its delegates: the one delegate from Argentina or Japan consequently held equal voting power to the scores or even hundreds from France or Germany. But gradually the organisation was tightened up, and in 1907 a scheme was adopted which gave twenty votes each to the leading nations, and proportionately fewer to the others. Moreover a permanent Bureau was established at Brussels, with Emile Vandervelde, the distinguished leader of the Belgian Socialists, later well known in England as the Ministerial representative of the Belgian Government during the war, as

Chairman. In England, where the Socialist and Trade Union forces were divided, it was necessary to constitute a special joint committee in order to raise the British quota of the cost of the Bureau, and to elect and instruct the British delegates. It was decided by the Brussels Bureau that the 20 British votes should be allotted, 10 to the Labour Party, 4 to the I.L.P., 4 to the British Socialist Party (into which the old S.D.F. had merged), and 2 to the Fabian Society, and the British Section of the International Socialist Bureau was, and still remains, constituted financially and electorally on that basis.

In France and in several other countries the internal differences between sections of the Socialist Party have been carried to far greater lengths than have ever been known in England. In France there have been hostile groups of Socialist representatives in the Chamber of Deputies and constant internecine opposition in electoral campaigns. In Great Britain the rivalry of different societies has consisted for the most part in separate schemes of propaganda, in occasional bickerings in their publications, in squabbles over local elections, and sometimes over the selection but not the election of parliamentary candidates. On the other hand co-operation on particular problems and exchange of courtesies have been common.

The International Socialist Bureau, under instructions from the Copenhagen Conference had made a successful attempt to unite the warring elements of French Socialism, and in the autumn of 1912 the three British Socialist Societies were approached with a view to a conference with the Bureau on the subject of Socialist unity in Great Britain. Convenient dates could not be fixed, and the matter was dropped, but in July, 1913, M. Vandervelde, the Chairman, and M. Camille Huysmans, the Secretary of the Bureau, came over from Brussels and a hurried meeting of delegates assembled in the Fabian office to discuss their proposals. The Bureau had the good sense to recognise that the way to unity led through the Labour Party; and it was agreed that the three Socialist bodies should form a United Socialist Council, subject to the condition that the British Socialist Party should affiliate to the Labour Party.

In December, 1913, a formal conference was held in London, attended on this occasion by all the members of the International Socialist Bureau, representing the Socialist parties of twenty different countries. The crux of the question was to find a form of words which satisfied all susceptibilities; and Sidney Webb, who was chosen chairman of a part of the proceedings when the British delegates met by themselves to formulate the terms of agreement, was here in his element; for it would be hard to find anybody in England more skilful in solving the difficulties that arise in determining the expression of a proposition of which the substance is not in dispute.

An agreement was arrived at that the Joint Socialist Council should be formed as soon as the British Socialist Party was affiliated to the Labour Party. The B.S.P. confirmed the decision of its delegates, but the Labour Party referred the acceptance of affiliation to the Annual Conference of 1915.

Then came the War. The Labour Party Conference of 1915 did not take place, and a sudden new divergence of opinion arose in the Socialist movement. The Labour Party, the Fabian Society, and the leaders of the B.S.P. gave general support to the Government in entering into the war. The I.L.P. adopted an attitude of critical hostility. Amidst this somewhat unexpected regrouping of parties, any attempt to inaugurate a United Socialist Council was foredoomed to failure. The project for Socialist Unity therefore awaits the happy time when war shall have ceased.

Chapter XI   The Minority Report, Syndicalism and Research: 1909-15

The emergence of Mrs. Sidney Webb – The Poor Law Commission – The Minority Report – Unemployment – The National Committee for the Prevention of Destitution – "Vote against the House of Lords" – Bernard Shaw retires – Death of Hubert Bland – Opposition to the National Insurance Bill – The Fabian Reform Committee – The "New Statesman" – The Research Department – "The Rural Problem" – "The Control of Industry" – Syndicalism – The Guildsmen – Final Statistics – The War.

A former chapter was entitled "The Episode of Mr. Wells." The present might have been called "The Intervention of Mrs. Sidney Webb," save for the fact that it would suggest a comparison which might be misleading.

I have insisted with some iteration that the success of the Society, both in its early days and afterwards, must be mainly attributed to the exceptional force and ability of the Essayists. Later in its history only two persons have come forward who are in my opinion entitled in their Fabian work to rank with the original leaders, to wit, Mr. Wells and Mrs. Webb. Of the former I have said enough already. The present chapter will be largely devoted to the influence of the latter.

It must however be observed that in all their achievements it is impossible to make a clear distinction between Mrs. Webb and her husband. For example, the Minority Report of the Poor Law

Commission, shortly to be dealt with, purported to be the work of Mrs. Webb and her three co-signatories. In fact the investigation, the invention, and the conclusions were in the fullest sense joint, although the draft which went to the typist was in the handwriting of Mr. Webb. On some occasions at any rate Mrs. Webb lectures from notes in her husband's eminently legible handwriting: her own — oddly unlike her character — is indecipherable without prolonged scrutiny even by herself. Sometimes, on the other hand, it is possible to separate the work of the two. Mrs. Webb, although elected a member in 1893, took practically no part in the Fabian Society until 1906. It may be said, with substantial if not literal accuracy, that her only contributions to the Society for the first dozen years of her membership were a couple of lectures and Tract No. 67, "Women and the Factory Acts." The Suffrage movement and the Wells episode brought her to our meetings, and her lecture in "The Faith I Hold" series, a description of her upbringing amongst the captains of industry who built some of the world's great railways, was amongst the most memorable in the long Fabian series. Still she neither held nor sought any official position; and the main work of a Society is necessarily done by the few who sit at its Committees often twice or thrice a week.

The transformation of Mrs. Webb from a student and writer, a typical "socialist of the chair," into an active leader and propagandist originated in December, 1905, when she was appointed a member of the Royal Commission on the Poor Law. The Fabian Society had nothing to do with the Commission during its four years of enquiry, though as usual not a few Fabians took part in the work, both officially and unofficially. But when in the spring of 1909 the Minority Report was issued, signed by Mrs. Webb and George Lansbury, both members of the Society, as well as by the Rev. Russell Wakefield (now the Bishop of Birmingham) and Mr. F. Chandler, Secretary of the Amalgamated Society of Carpenters and Joiners, the Society took it up. Mr. and Mrs. Webb reprinted the Minority Report with an introduction and notes in two octavo volumes, and they lent the Society the plates for a paper edition in two parts at a shilling and two shillings, one dealing with Unemployment and the other with the reconstruction of the Poor Law, some 6000 copies of which were sold at a substantial profit.

The Treasury Solicitor was rash enough to threaten us with an injunction on the ground of infringement of the Crown copyright and to demand an instant withdrawal of our edition. But Government Departments which try conclusions with the Fabian Society generally find the Society better informed than themselves; and we were able triumphantly to refer the Treasury Solicitor to a published declaration of his own employers, the Lords Commissioners of the Treasury, a score of years before, in which they expressly disclaimed their privilege of copyright monopoly so far as ordinary blue books were concerned, and actually encouraged the reprinting of them for the public advantage. And, with characteristic impudence, we intimated also that, if the Government wished to try the issue, it might find that the legal copyright was not in the Crown at all, as the actual writer of the Report, to whom alone the law gives copyright, had never ceded his copyright and was not a member of the Royal Commission at all! At the same time we prepared to get the utmost advertisement out of the attempt to suppress the popular circulation of the Report, and we made this fact known to the Prime Minister. In the end the Treasury Solicitor had to climb down and withdraw his objection. What the Government did was to undercut us by publishing a still cheaper edition, which did not stop our sales, and thus the public benefited by our enterprise, and an enormous circulation was obtained for the Report.

The Minority Report of the Poor Law Commission—although never, from first to last, mentioning Socialism—was a notable and wholly original addition to Socialist theory, entirely of Fabian origin. Hitherto all Socialist writings on the organisation of society, whether contemporary or Utopian, had visualised a world composed exclusively of healthy, sane, and effective citizens, mostly adults. No Socialist had stopped to think out how, in a densely populated and highly industrialised Socialist community, we should provide systematically for the orphans, the sick, the physically or mentally defective and the aged on the one hand, and for the adults for whom at any time no immediate employment could be found. The Minority Report, whilst making immediately practicable proposals for the reform of all the evils of the Poor Law, worked out the lines along which the necessary organisation must proceed, even in the fully socialised State. We had, in the Fabian Society, made attempts to deal with both sides of this problem; but our publications, both on the Poor Law and on the Unemployed, had lacked the foundation of solid fact and the discovery of new principles, which the four years' work of the Fabians connected with the Poor Law Commission now supplied.

English Socialists have always paid great and perhaps excessive attention to the problem of unemployment. Partly this is due to the fact that Socialism came to the front in Great Britain at a period when unemployment was exceptionally rife, and when for the first time in the nineteenth century the community had become acutely aware of it. In our early days it was commonly believed to be a rapidly growing evil. Machinery was replacing men: the capitalists would employ a few hands to turn the machines on and off: wealth would be produced for the rich, and most of the present manual working class would become superfluous. The only reply, so far as I know, to this line of argumentative forecast is that it does not happen. The world is at present so avid of wealth, so eager for more things to use or consume, that however quickly iron and copper replace flesh and blood, the demand for men keeps pace with it. Anyway, unemployment in the twentieth century has so far been less prevalent than it was in the nineteenth, and nobody now suggests, as did Mrs. Besant in 1889, that the increasing army of the unemployed, provided with work by the State, would ultimately oust the employees of private capitalism. Unemployment in fact is at least as old as the days of Queen Elizabeth, when the great Poor Law of 1601 was passed to cope with it. Whilst labour was scattered and the artisan still frequently his own master, unemployment was indefinite and relatively imperceptible. When masses of men and women came to be employed in factories, the closing of the factory made unemployment obvious to those on the spot. But two generations ago Lancashire and Yorkshire were far away from London, and the nation as a whole knew little and cared less about hard times amongst cotton operatives or iron-workers in the remote north.

It may be said with fair accuracy that Unemployment was scarcely recognised as a social problem before the last quarter of the nineteenth century, though in fact it had existed for centuries, and had been prevalent for fifty years. Mill in his "Political Economy," which treats so sympathetically of the state of labour under capitalism, has no reference to it in the elaborate table of contents. Indeed the word unemployment is so recent as to have actually been unknown before the early nineties.

But the Trade Unionists had always been aware of unemployment, since, after strike pay, it is "out-of-work benefit" which they have found the best protection for the standard rate of wages, and nothing in the program of Socialism appealed to them more directly than its claim to abolish unemployment. Finally it may be said that unemployment is on the whole more prevalent in Great Britain than elsewhere; the system of casual or intermittent employment is more widespread; throughout the Continent the working classes in towns are nearly everywhere connected with the rural peasant landowners or occupiers, so that the town labourer can often go back to the land at any rate for his keep; whilst all America, still predominantly agricultural, is in something like a similar case.

The Fabian Society had since its earliest days been conscious of the problem of unemployment; but it had done little to solve it. The "Report on the Government Organisation of Unemployed Labour," printed "for the information of members" in 1886, had been long forgotten, and an attempt to revise it made some time in the nineties had come to nothing. In "Fabian Essays" unemployment is rightly recognised as the Achilles heel of the proletarian system, but the practical problem is not solved or even thoroughly understood; the plausible error of supposing that the unemployed baker and bootmaker can be set to make bread and boots for one another still persists. In 1893 we reprinted from the "Nineteenth Century" as Tract No. 47 a paper on "The Unemployed" by John Burns, and we had published nothing else.

In fact we found the subject too difficult. There were plenty of palliatives familiar to every social enquirer; Socialism, the organisation of industry by the community for the community, we regarded as the real and final remedy. But between the former, such as labour bureaux, farm colonies, afforestation, the eight hours day, which admittedly were at best only partial and temporary, and Socialism, which was obviously far off, there was a great gulf fixed, and how to bridge it we knew not. At last the Minority Report provided an answer. It was a comprehensive and practicable scheme for preventing unemployment under existing conditions, and for coping with the mass of incompetent destitution which for generations had been the disgrace of our civilisation.

Into the details of this scheme I must not enter because it is, properly speaking, outside the scope of this book. The propaganda for carrying the Report into effect was undertaken by the National Committee for the Prevention of Destitution, established by Mrs. Webb as a separate organisation. The necessity for this step was significant of the extent to which Socialism, as it crystallises into practical measures, invades the common body of British thought. People who would not dream of calling themselves Socialists, much less contributing to the funds of a Socialist Society, become enthusiastically interested in separate parts of its program as soon as it has a program, provided these parts are presented on their own merits and not as approaches to Socialism. Indeed many who regard Socialism as a menace to society are so anxious to find and support alternatives to it, that they will endow expensive Socialistic investigations and subscribe to elaborate Socialistic schemes of reform under the impression that nothing that is thoughtful, practical, well informed, and constitutional can possibly have any connection with the Red Spectre which stands in their imagination for Socialism. To such people the Minority Report, a document obviously the work of highly skilled and disinterested political thinkers and experts, would recommend itself as the constitutional basis of a Society for the Prevention of Destitution: that is, of the condition which not only smites the conscientious rich with a compunction that no special pleading by arm-chair economists can allay, but which offers a hotbed to the sowers of Socialism. Add to these the considerable number of convinced or half-convinced Socialists who for various reasons are not in a position to make a definite profession of Socialism without great inconvenience, real or imaginary, to themselves, and it will be plain that Mrs. Webb would have been throwing away much of her available resources if she had not used the device of a new organisation to agitate for the Minority Report *ad hoc*.

Many Fabians served on the Committee—indeed a large proportion of our members must have taken part in its incessant activities—and the relations between the two bodies were close; but most of the subscribers to the Committee and many of its most active members came from outside the Society, and were in no way committed to its general principles.

For two whole years Mrs. Webb managed her Committee with great vigour and dash. She collected for it a considerable income and a large number of workers: she lectured and organised all over the country; she discovered that she was an excellent propagandist, and that what she could do with success she also did with zest.

In the summer of 1911 Mr. and Mrs. Webb left England for a tour round the world, and Mrs. Webb had mentioned before she left that she was willing to be nominated for the Executive. At the election in

April, 1912, whilst still abroad, she was returned second on the poll, with 778 votes, only a dozen behind her husband.

From this point onwards Mrs. Webb has been on the whole the dominant personality in the Society. This does not necessarily mean that she is abler or stronger than her husband or Bernard Shaw. But the latter had withdrawn from the Executive Committee, and the former, with the rest of the Old Gang, had made the Society what it already was. Mrs. Webb brought a fresh and fertile mind to its councils. Her twenty years of membership and intimate private acquaintance with its leaders made her familiar with its possibilities, but she was free from the influence of past failures—in such matters for example as Socialist Unity—and she was eager to start out on new lines which the almost unconscious traditions of the Society had hitherto barred.

The story of the Society has been traced to the conclusion of the intervention of Mr. Wells, and I then turned aside to describe the numerous new activities of the booming years which followed the Labour Party triumph of 1906. I must now complete the history of the internal affairs of the Society.

As a political body, the Society has usually, though not invariably, issued some sort of pronouncement on the eve of a General Election. In January, 1910, the Executive Committee published in "Fabian News" a brief manifesto addressed to the members urging them to "Vote against the House of Lords." It will be recollected that the Lords had rejected the Budget, and the sole issue before the country was the right of the House of Commons to control finance. Members were urged to support any duly accredited Labour or socialist candidate; elsewhere they were, in effect, advised to vote for the Liberal candidates. In April their action in publishing this "Special advice to members" without the consent of a members' meeting was challenged, but the Executive Committee's contention that it was entitled to advise the members, and that the advice given was sound, was endorsed by a very large majority.

At the Annual Meeting the Executive Committee, with a view to setting forth once more their reasoned view on a subject of perennial trouble to new members, accepted a resolution instructing them to consider and report on the advisability of limiting the liberty of members to support political parties other than Labour or Socialist, and on November 4th R.C.K. Ensor on behalf of the Executive gave an admirable address on Fabian Policy. He explained that the Society had never set out to become a political party, and that in this respect it differed in the most marked manner from most Socialist bodies. Its collective support of the Labour Party combined with toleration of Liberals suited a world of real men who can seldom be arranged on tidy and geometrical lines. This report was accepted by general consent, and in December, when Parliament was again dissolved, this time on the question of the Veto of the Lords, the Executive repeated their "Advice to Members" to vote for Liberals whenever no properly accredited Labour or Socialist candidate was in the field.

But the dissatisfaction with the old policy, and with its old exponents, was not yet dispelled. A new generation was knocking at the door, and some of the old leaders thought that the time had come to make room for them. Hubert Bland was suffering from uncertain health, and he made up his mind to retire from the official positions he had held since the formation of the Society. Bernard Shaw determined to join him and then suggested the same course to the rest of his contemporaries. Some of them concurred, and in addition to the two already named R.C.K. Ensor (who returned a year later), Stewart Headlam, and George Standring withdrew from the Executive in order to make room for younger members. Twenty-two new candidates came forward at the election of April, 1911; but on the whole the Society showed no particular eagerness for change. The retiring members were re-elected ahead of all the new ones, with Sidney Webb at the top of the poll, and the five additions to the Executive, Emil Davies, Mrs. C.M. Wilson, Reginald Bray, L.C.C., Mrs. F. Cavendish Bentinck, and Henry D. Harben, were none of them exactly youthful or ardent innovators.

By this time it was apparent that the self-denying ordinance of the veterans was not really necessary, and the Executive, loath to lose the stimulation of Shaw's constant presence, devised a scheme to authorise the elected members to co-opt as consultative members persons who had already held office for ten years and had retired. The Executive itself was by no means unanimous on this policy, and at the Annual Meeting one of them, Henry H. Slesser, led the opposition to any departure from "the principles of pure democracy." On a show of hands the proposal appeared to be defeated by a small majority, and in the face of the opposition was withdrawn. This is almost the only occasion on which the Executive Committee have failed to carry their policy through the Society, and they might have succeeded even in this instance, either at the meeting or on a referendum, if they had chosen to insist on an alteration in the constitution against the wishes of a substantial fraction of the membership.

Here then it may be said that the rule of the essayists as a body came to an end. Sidney Webb alone remained in office. Hubert Bland was in rapidly declining health. Only once again he addressed the Society, on July 16th, 1912, when he examined the history of "Fabian Policy," and indicated the changes which he thought should be made to adapt it to new conditions. Soon after this his sight completely failed, and in April, 1914, he died suddenly of long-standing heart disease.

Bernard Shaw happily for the Society has not ceased to concern himself in its activities, although he is no longer officially responsible for their management. His freedom from office does not always make the task of his successors easier. The loyalest of colleagues, he had always defended their policy, whether or not it was exactly of his own choice; but in his capacity of private member his unrivalled influence is occasionally something of a difficulty. If he does not happen to approve of what the Executive proposes he can generally persuade a Business Meeting to vote for something else!

At this same period, the spring of 1911, the National Insurance Bill was introduced. This was a subject to which the Society had given but little attention and on which it had not formulated a policy. It had opposed the contributory system as proposed to be applied to Old Age Pensions, and a paper on "Paupers and Old Age Pensions," published by Sidney Webb in the "Albany Review" in August, 1907, and reprinted by the Society as Tract No. 135, had probably much influence in deciding the Government to abandon its original plan of excluding paupers permanently from the scheme by showing what difficulties and anomalies would follow from any such course. The National Insurance Bill when first introduced was severely criticised by Sidney Webb in documents circulated amongst Trade Unionists and published in various forms; but a few weeks later he started on his tour round the world and could take no further part in the affair. At the Annual Conference of Fabian Societies in July, 1911, an amendment proposed by H.D. Harben to a resolution dealing with the Bill was carried against a small minority. The amendment declared that the Bill should be opposed, and in furtherance of the policy thus casually suggested and irregularly adopted, the Executive Committee joined with a section of the I.L.P. in a vigorous campaign to defeat the Bill. This was a new rôle for the Society. Usually it has adopted the principle of accepting and making the best of what has already happened; and in politics a Bill introduced by a strong Government is a *fait accompli*; it is too late to say that something else would have been preferable. It may be amended: it may possibly be withdrawn: it cannot be exchanged for another scheme.

I shall not however dwell on this episode in Fabian history because for once I was in complete disagreement with all my colleagues, except Sir Leo Chiozza Money, and perhaps I cannot yet view the matter with entire detachment. The Labour Party decided to meet the Bill with friendly criticism, to recognise it as a great measure of social reform, and to advocate amendments which they deemed improvements. The Fabian Society attacked the Bill with hostile amendments, prophesied all sorts of calamities as certain to result from it: magnified its administrative difficulties, and generally encouraged the duchesses and farmers who passively resisted it; but their endeavour to defeat the Bill was a failure.

It may be too soon to be confident that the policy of the Society in this matter was wrong. But the Trade Unions are stronger than ever: the Friendly Societies are not bankrupt: the working people are insured against sickness: and anybody who now proposed to repeal the Act would be regarded as a lunatic.

Meanwhile the withdrawal of some of the older had by no means satisfied the younger generation, and during the autumn of 1911 a Fabian Reform Committee was constituted, with Henry H. Slesser as Chairman, Dr. Marion Phillips as Vice-Chairman, Clifford Allen as Secretary, and fifteen other members, including Dr. Ethel Bentham, who, like Mr. Slesser, was a member of the Executive. Their programme, like that of Mr. Wells, included a number of reforms of procedure, none of them of much consequence; and a political policy, which was to insist "that if Fabians do take part in politics, they should do so only as supporters of the Labour Party." The campaign of the Committee lasted a year, and as usual in such cases led to a good deal of somewhat heated controversy over matters which now appear to be very trivial. It is therefore not worth while to recount the details of the proceedings, which can be found by any enquirer in the pages of "Fabian News." Two of the leaders, Dr. Marion Phillips and Clifford Allen, were elected to the Executive at the election of 1912, and some of the administrative reforms proposed by the Committee were carried into effect. The Reformers elected to fight the battle of political policy on point of detail, until in July, 1912, the Executive Committee resolved to bring the matter to an issue, and to that end moved at a members' meeting: "That this meeting endorses the constitutional practice of the Society which accords complete toleration to its members; and whilst reaffirming its loyalty to the Labour Party, to which party alone it as a society has given support, it declines to interfere ... with the right of each member to decide on the manner in which he can best work for Socialism in accordance with his individual opportunities and circumstances." (The phrase omitted refers to the rule about expulsion of members, a safeguard which in fact has never been resorted to.) An amendment of the Reformers embodying their policy was defeated by 122 to 27 and after the holiday season the Reform Committed announced that their mission was accomplished and their organisation had been disbanded.

"Fabian Reform" embodied no new principle. All through the history of the Society there had been a conflict between the "constitutional practice" of political toleration, and the desire of a militant minority to set up a standard of party orthodoxy, and to penalise or expel the dissenters from it.

The next storm which disturbed Fabian equanimity involved an altogether new principle, and was therefore a refreshing change to the veterans, who were growing weary of winning battles fought over the same ground. In order to explain this movement it is necessary to describe a new development in the work of the Society.

In the autumn of 1912 Mrs. Webb came to the conclusion that the work of the National Committee for the Prevention of Destitution could not be carried on indefinitely on a large scale. Reform of the Poor Law was not coming as a big scheme. It was true that the Majority Report was almost forgotten, but there appeared to be no longer any hope that the Government would take up as a whole the scheme of the Minority Report. It would come about in due time, but not as the result of an agitation. The National Committee had a monthly paper, "The Crusade," edited by Clifford Sharp, a member of the Society who came to the front at the time of the Wells agitation, had been one of the founders of the Nursery, and a member of the Executive from 1909 to 1914. In March, 1913, Bernard Shaw, H.D.

Harben, and the Webbs, with a few other friends, established the "New Statesman," with Clifford Sharp as editor. This weekly review is not the organ of the Society, and is not in any formal way connected with it, but none the less it does in fact express the policy which has moulded the Society, and it has been a useful vehicle for publishing the results of Fabian Research.

Fabian Research, the other outgrowth of the Committee for the Prevention of Destitution, was organised by Mrs. Webb in the autumn of 1912. Investigation of social problems was one of the original objects of the Society and had always been a recognised part of its work. As a general rule, members had taken it up individually, but at various periods Committees had been appointed to investigate particular subjects. The important work of one of these Committees, on the Decline of the Birth-rate, has been described in an earlier chapter. Mrs. Webb's plan was to systematise research, to enlist the co-operation of social enquirers not necessarily committed to the principles of the Society, and to obtain funds for this special purpose from those who would not contribute to the political side of the Society's operations.

The "Committees of Inquiry" then formed took up two subjects, the "Control of Industry" and "Land Problems and Rural Development." The latter was organised by H.D. Harben and was carried on independently. After a large amount of information had been collected, partly in writing and partly from the oral evidence of specialists, a Report was drafted by Mr. Harben and published first as a Supplement to the "New Statesman" on August 4th, 1913, and some months later by Messrs. Constable for the Fabian Society as a half-a-crown volume entitled "The Rural Problem."

In fact there is a consensus of opinion throughout all parties on this group of questions. Socialists, Liberals, and a large section of Conservatives advocate Wages Boards for providing a statutory minimum wage for farm labourers, State aid for building of cottages and a resolute speeding up in the provision of land for small holdings. The Fabian presentment of the case did not substantially differ from that of the Land Report published a few months later under Liberal auspices, and our Report, though useful, cannot be said to have been epoch-making.

Meanwhile the Enquiry into the Control of Industry was developing on wider lines. The Research Department set up its own office and staff, and began to collect information about all the methods of control of industry at present existing as alternatives to the normal capitalist system. Co-operation in all its forms, the resistances of Trade Unionism, the effects of professional organisations, such as those of the Teachers and of the Engineers, and all varieties of State and Municipal enterprise, were investigated in turn; several reports have been published as "New Statesman" Supplements, and a volume or series of volumes will in due time appear.

The problem of the Control of Industry had become important because of the rise of a new school of thought amongst Socialists, especially in France, where the rapid growth of Trade Unionism since 1884, combined with profound distrust of the group system of party politics, had led to a revival of old-fashioned anarchism in a new form. Syndicalism, which is the French word for Trade Unionism, proposes that the future State should be organised on the basis of Trade Unions; it regards a man's occupation as more vitally important to him than his place of residence, and therefore advocates representation by trades in place of localities: it lays stress on his desire, his right, to control his own working life directly through his own elected representatives of his trade: it criticises the "servile state" proposed by collectivists, wherein the workman, it is said, would be a wage-slave to officials of the State, as he is now to officials of the capitalists. Thus it proposes that the control of industry should be in the hands of the producers, and not, as at present, in the hands of consumers through capitalists catering for their custom, or through co-operative societies of consumers, or through the State acting on behalf of citizens who are consumers.

A quite extraordinary diversity of streams of opinion converged to give volume to this new trend of thought. There was the literary criticism of Mr. Hilaire Belloc, whose ideal is the peasant proprietor of France, freed from governmental control, a self-sufficient producer of all his requirements. His attack was directed against the Servile State, supposed to be foreshadowed by the Minority Report, which proposed drastic collective control over the derelicts of our present social anarchy. Then Mr. Tom Mann came back from Australia as the prophet of the new proletarian gospel, and for a few months attracted working-class attention by his energy and eloquence. The South Wales miners, after many years of acquiescence in the rule of successful and highly respected but somewhat old-fashioned leaders, were awakening to a sense of power, and demanding from their

Unions a more aggressive policy. The parliamentary Labour Party since 1910 had resolved to support the Liberal Government in its contest with the House of Lords and in its demand for Irish Home Rule, and as Labour support was essential to the continuance of the Liberals in power, they were debarred from pushing their own proposals regardless of consequences. Although therefore the party was pledged to the demand for Women's Franchise, they refused to wreck the Government on its behalf. Hence impatient Socialists and extreme Suffragists united in proclaiming that the Labour Party was no longer of any use, and that "direct action" by Suffragettes and Trade Unionists was the only method of progress. The "Daily Herald," a newspaper started by a group of compositors in London, was acquired by partisans of this policy, and as long as it lived incessantly derided the Labour Party and advocated Women's Franchise and some sort of Syndicalism as the social panacea. Moreover a variant on Syndicalism, of a more reasoned and less revolutionary character, called "Guild Socialism," was proposed by Mr. A.R. Orage in the pages of his weekly, "The New Age," and gained a following especially in Oxford, where Mr. G.D.H. Cole was leader of the University Fabian Society. His book on Trade Unionism, entitled "The World of Labour," published at the end of 1913, attracted much attention, and he threw himself with great energy into the Trade Union enquiry of the Research Department, of which his friend and ally, Mr. W. Mellor, was the Secretary. Mr. Cole was elected to the Executive Committee in April, 1914, and soon afterwards began a new "Reform" movement. He had become a prophet of the "Guild Socialism" school, and was at that time extremely hostile to the Labour Party. Indeed a year before, when dissatisfaction with the party was prevalent, he had proposed at a business meeting that the Fabian Society should disaffiliate, but he had failed to carry his resolution by 92 votes against 48. In the summer of 1914 however he arrived at an understanding with Mr. Clifford Allen, also a member of the Executive, and with other out and out supporters of the Labour Party, by which they agreed to combine their altogether inconsistent policies into a single new program for the Fabian Society. The program of the "several schools of thought," published in "Fabian News" for April, 1915, laid down that the object of the Society should be to carry out research, that the Basis should be replaced merely by the phrase, "The Fabian Society consists of Socialists and forms part of the national and international movement for the emancipation of the community from the capitalist system"; and that a new rule should be adopted forbidding members to belong to, or publicly to associate with, any organisation opposed to that movement of which this Society had declared itself a part. The Executive Committee published a lengthy rejoinder, and at the election of the Executive Committee a few weeks later the members by their votes clearly indicated their disapproval of the new scheme. At the Annual Meeting in May, 1915, only small minorities supported the plan of reconstruction, and Mr. Cole then and there resigned his membership of the Society, and was subsequently followed by a few other members. A little while later the Oxford University Fabian Society severed its connection with the parent Society, and Mr. Cole adopted the wise course of founding a society of his own for the advocacy of Guild Socialism.

This episode brings the history of the Society down to the present date, and I shall conclude this chapter with a brief account of its organisation at the time of writing, the summer of 1915.

At the end of 1913 my own long term of service as chief officer of the Society came to an end, and my colleague for several previous years, W. Stephen Sanders, was appointed my successor. The Executive Committee requested me to take the new office of Honorary Secretary, and to retain a share in the management of the Society. This position I still hold.

The tide of Socialist progress which began to rise in 1905 had turned before 1914, and the period of depression was intensified by the war, which is still the dominant fact in the world. The membership of the Society reached its maximum in 1913, 2804 in the parent Society and about 500 others in local societies. In 1915 the members were 2588 and 250. The removal to new premises in the autumn of 1914 was more than a mere change of offices, since it provided the Society with a shop for the sale of its publications, a hall sufficiently large for minor meetings, and accommodation in the same house for the Research Department and the Women's Group. Moreover a couple of rooms were furnished as a "Common Room" for members, in which light refreshments can be obtained and Socialist publications consulted. The finances of the Society have of course been adversely affected by the war, but not, so far, to a very material extent.

The chief new departure of recent years has been the organisation of courses of lectures in London for the general public by Bernard

Shaw, Sidney Webb, and Mrs. Webb, which have not only been of value as a means of propaganda, but have also yielded a substantial profit for the purposes of the Society. The plan originated with a debate between Bernard Shaw and G.K. Chesterton in 1911, which attracted a crowded audience and much popular interest. Next year Mr. Shaw debated with Mr. Hilaire Belloc: in 1913 Mr. and Mrs. Webb gave six lectures at King's Hall on "Socialism Restated": in 1914 Bernard Shaw gave another course of six at Kingsway Hall on the "Redistribution of Income," in which he developed the thesis that the economic goal of Socialism is equality of income for all. Lastly, in 1915 a course of six lectures at King's Hall by the three already named on "The World after the War" proved to be unexpectedly successful. The lecturing to clubs and other societies carried on by new generations of members still continues, but it forms by no means so prominent a part of the Society's work as in earlier years.

Local Fabian organisation, as is always the case in time of depression, is on the down grade. The London groups scarcely exist, and but few local societies, besides that of Liverpool, show signs of life. The Research Department, the Women's Group, and the Nursery are still active.

The Society has an old-established tradition and a settled policy, but in fact it is not now controlled by anything like an Old Gang. The Executive Committee numbers twenty-one: two only of these, Sidney Webb and myself, have sat upon it from its early days: only two others, Dr. Lawson Dodd (the Treasurer) and W. Stephen Sanders (the General Secretary) were on the Executive during the great contest with Mr. Wells ten years ago. All the rest have joined it within the last few years, and if they support the old tradition, it is because they accept it, and not because they created it. Moreover the majority of the members are young people, most of them born since the Society was founded. The Society is old, but it does not consist, in the main, of old people.

What its future may be I shall consider in the next, and concluding, chapter.

I must add a final paragraph to my history. At the time I write, in the first days of 1916, the war is with us and the end is not in sight. In accordance with the rule which forbids it to speak, unless it has something of value to say, the Society has made no pronouncement and adopted no policy. A resolution registering the opinion of the majority of a few hundred members assembled in a hall is not worth recording when the subject is one in which millions are as concerned and virtually as competent as themselves.

Naturally there is diversity of opinion amongst the members. On the one hand Mr. Clifford Allen, a member of the Executive, has played a leading part in organising opposition to conscription and opposing the policy of the Government. On the other hand two other members of the Executive Committee, Mr. H.J. Gillespie and Mr. C.M. Lloyd, have, since the beginning of the war, resigned their seats in order to take commissions in the Army. Another member, the General Secretary, after months of vigorous service as one of the Labour Party delegates to Lord Derby's Recruiting Committee, accepted a commission in the Army in November, 1915, in order to devote his whole time to this work, and has been granted leave of absence for the period of the war, whilst I have undertaken my old work in his place. Many members of the Society joined the Army in the early months of the war, and already a number, amongst whom may be named Rupert Brooke, have given their lives for their country.

Chapter XII   The Lessons of Thirty Years

Breaking the spell of Marxism – A French verdict – Origin of Revisionism in Germany – The British School of Socialism – Mr. Ernest Barker's summary – Mill versus Marx – The Fabian Method – Making Socialists or making Socialism – The life of propagandist societies – The prospects of Socialist Unity – The future of Fabian ideas – The test of Fabian success.

The Fabian Society was founded for the purpose of reconstructing Society in accordance with the highest moral possibilities. This is still the most accurate and compendious description of its object and the nature of its work. But the stage of idealism at which more than a very modest instalment of this cosmic process seemed possible within the lifetime of a single institution had passed before the chief Essayists became members, and indeed I cannot recollect that the founders themselves ever imagined that it lay within their own power to reconstruct Society; none of them was really so sanguine or so self-confident as to anticipate so great a result from their efforts, and it will be remembered that the original phrase was altered by the insertion of the words "to help on" when the constitution was actually formulated. Society has not yet been reconstructed, but the Fabians have done something towards its reconstruction, and my history will be incomplete without an attempt to indicate what the Society has already accomplished and what may be the future of its work.

Its first achievement, as already mentioned, was to break the spell of Marxism in England. Public opinion altogether failed to recognise the greatness of Marx during his lifetime, but every year that passes adds strength to the conviction that the broad principles he promulgated will guide the evolution of society during the present century. Marx demonstrated the moral bankruptcy of commercialism and formulated the demand for the communal ownership and organisation of industry; and it is hardly possible to exaggerate the value of this service to humanity. But no man is great enough to be made into a god; no man, however wise, can see far into the future. Neither Marx himself nor his immediate followers recognised the real basis of his future fame; they thought he was a brilliant and original economist, and a profound student of history. His Theory of Value, his Economic Interpretation of History, seemed to them the incontestible premises which necessarily led to his political conclusions. This misapprehension would not have much mattered had they allowed themselves freedom of thought. Socialism, as first preached to the English people by the Social Democrats, was as narrow, as bigoted, as exclusive as the strictest of Scotch religious sects. *Das Kapital*, Vol. I, was its bible; and the thoughts and schemes of English Socialists were to be approved or condemned according as they could or could not be justified by a quoted text.

The Fabian Society freed English Socialism from this intellectual bondage, and freed it sooner and more completely than "Revisionists" have succeeded in doing anywhere else.

Accepting the great principle that the reconstruction of society to be worked for is the ownership and control of industry by the community, the Fabians refused to regard as articles of faith either the economic and historic analyses which Marx made use of or the political evolution which he predicted.

Socialism in England remained the fantastic creed of a group of fanatics until "Fabian Essays" and the Lancashire Campaign taught the working classes of England, or at any rate their leaders, that Socialism was a living principle which could be applied to existing social and political conditions without a cataclysm either insurrectionary or even political. Revolutionary phraseology, the language of violence, survived, and still survives, just as in ordinary politics we use the metaphors of warfare and pretend that the peaceful polling booth is a battlefield and that our political opponents are hostile armies. But we only wave the red flag in our songs, and we recognise nowadays that the real battles of Socialism are fought in committee rooms at Westminster and in the council chambers of Town Halls.

It was perhaps fortunate that none of the Fabian leaders came within the influence of the extraordinary personality of Karl Marx. Had he lived a few years longer he might have dominated them as he dominated his German followers, and one or two of his English adherents. Then years would have been wasted in the struggle to escape. It was fortunate also that the Fabian Society has never possessed one single outstanding leader, and has always refrained from electing a president or permanent chairman. There never has been a Fabian orthodoxy, because no one was in a position to assert what the true faith was.

Freedom of thought was without doubt obtained for English Socialists by the Fabians. How far the world-wide revolt against Marxian orthodoxy had its origin in England is another and more difficult question. In his study of the Fabian Society M. Édouard Pfeiffer states in the preface that the Society makes this claim, quotes Bernard Shaw as saying to him, "The world has been thoroughly Fabianised in the last twenty-five years," and adds that he is going to examine the accuracy of it. Later he says:

"The Fabians were the first amongst Socialists to start the movement of anti-Marxist criticism. At a period when the dogmas of the Master were regarded as sacred, the Fabians ventured to assert that it was possible to call oneself a Socialist without ever having read *Das Kapital*, or without accepting its doctrine. In opposition to Marx, they have revived the spirit of J.S. Mill, and they have attacked Marx all along the line—the class war, the economic interpretation of history, the catastrophic method, and above all the theory of value."

This is a French view. Germany is naturally the stronghold of Marxism, and the country where it has proved, up to a point, an unqualified success. Although the Social Democratic Party was founded as an alliance between the followers of Marx and of Lassalle, on terms to which Marx himself violently objected, none the less the leadership of the party fell to those who accepted the teaching of Marx, and on that basis by far the greatest Socialist Party of the world has been built up. Nowhere else did the ideas of Marx hold such unquestioned supremacy: nowhere else had they such a body of loyal adherents, such a host of teachers and interpreters. Only on the question of agricultural land in the freer political atmosphere of South

Germany was there even a breath of dissent. The revolt came from England in the person of Edward Bernstein, who, exiled by Bismarck, took refuge in London, and was for years intimately acquainted with the Fabian Society and its leaders. Soon after his return to Germany he published in 1899 a volume criticising Marxism, and thence grew up the Revisionist movement for free thought in Socialism which has attracted all the younger men, and before the war had virtually, if not actually, obtained control over the Social Democratic Party.

In England, and in Germany through Bernstein, I think the Fabian Society may claim to have led the revolt. Elsewhere the revolt has come rather in deeds than in words. In France, in Italy, and in Belgium and in other European countries, a Socialist Party has grown up which amid greater political opportunities has had to face the actual problems of modern politics. These could not be solved by quotations from a German philosopher, and liberty has been gained by force of circumstances. Nevertheless in many countries, such as Russia and the United States, even now, or at any rate until very recent years, the freedom of action of Socialist parties has been impeded by excessive respect for the opinions of the Founder, and Socialist thought has been sterilised, because it was assumed that Marx had completed the philosophy of Socialism, and the business of Socialists was not to think for themselves, but merely to work for the realisation of his ideas.

But mere freedom was not enough. Something must be put in the place of Marx. His English followers did not notice that he had indicated no method, and devised no political machinery for the transition; or if they noticed it they passed over the omission as a negligible detail. If German Socialism would not suit, English Socialism had to be formulated to take its place. This has been the life-work of the Fabian Society, the working out of the application of the broad principles of Socialism to the industrial and political environment of England. I say England advisedly, because the industrial and political conditions of Scotland are in some degree different, and the application of the principles of Socialism to Ireland has not yet been seriously attempted. But for England "Fabian Essays" and the Fabian Tracts are by general consent the best expositions of the meaning and working of Socialism in the English language.

Marxian Socialism regarded itself as a thing apart. Marx had discovered a panacea for the ills of society: the old was to be cleared away and all things were to become new. In Marx's own thought evolution and revolution were tangled and alternated. The evolutionary side was essential to it; the idea of revolutionary catastrophe is almost an excrescence. But to the Marxians (of whom Marx once observed that he was not one) this excrescence became the whole thing. People were divided into those who advocated the revolution and those who did not. The business of propaganda was to increase the number of adherents of the new at the expense of the supporters of the old.

The Fabians regarded Socialism as a principle already in part embodied in the constitution of society, gradually extending its influence because it harmonised with the needs and desires of men in countries where the large industry prevails.

Fabian Socialism is in fact an interpretation of the spirit of the times. I have pointed out already that the municipalisation of monopolies, a typically Fabian process, had its origin decades before the Society was founded, and all that the Fabian Society did was to explain its social implications and advocate its wider extension. The same is true of the whole Fabian political policy. Socialism in English politics grew up because of the necessity for State intervention in the complex industrial and social organisation of a Great State. Almost before the evil results of Laissez Faire had culminated Robert Owen was pointing the way to factory legislation, popular education, and the communal care of children. The Ten Hours Act of 1847 was described by Marx himself as "the victory of a principle," that is, of "the political economy of the working class." That victory was frequently repeated in the next thirty years, and collective protection of Labour in the form of Factory Acts, Sanitary Acts, Truck Acts, Employers' Liability Acts, and Trade Board Acts became a recognised part of the policy of both political parties.

Fabian teaching has had more direct influence in promoting the administrative protection of Labour. The Fair Wages policy, now everywhere prevalent in State and Municipal employment, was, as has been already described, if not actually invented, at any rate largely popularised by the Society. It was a working-class demand, and it has been everywhere put forward by organised labour, but its success would have been slower had the manual workers been left to fight their own battle.

I have said that the work of the Society was the interpretation of an existing movement, the explanation and justification of tendencies which originated in Society at large, and not in societies, Fabian or other. That work is only less valuable than the formulation of new ideas. None of the Fabians would claim to rank beside the great promulgators of new ideas, such as Owen and Marx. But the interpretation of tendencies is necessary if progress is to be sustained and if it is to be unbroken by casual reaction. In an old country like ours, with vast forces of inertia built up by ages of precedents, by a class system which forms a part of the life of the nation, by a distribution of wealth which even yet scarcely yields to the pressure of graduated taxation, legislation is always in arrear of the needs of the times; the social structure is always old-fashioned and out of date, and reform always tends to be late, and even too late, unless there are agitators with the ability to attract public attention calling on the men in power to take action.

But this victory of a principle is not a complete victory of the principles of Socialism. It is a limitation of the power of the capitalist to use his capital as he pleases, and Socialism is much more than a series of social safeguards to the private ownership of capital. Municipal ownership is a further step, but even this will not carry us far because the capital suitable for municipal management on existing lines is but a small fraction of the whole, and because municipal control does not directly affect the amount of capital in the hands of the capitalists who are always expropriated with ample compensation.

We have made some progress along another line. Supertax, death duties, and taxes on unearned increment do a little to diminish the wealth of the few: old age pensions, national insurance, and workmen's compensation do something towards mitigating the poverty of the poor.

But it must be confessed that we have made but little progress along the main road of Socialism. Private ownership of capital and land flourishes almost as vigorously as it did thirty years ago. Its grosser cruelties have been checked, but the thing itself has barely been touched. Time alone will show whether progress is to be along existing lines, whether the power of the owners of capital over the wealth it helps to create and over the lives of the workers whom it enslaves will gradually fade away, as the power of our kings over the

Government of our country has faded, the form remaining when the substance has vanished, or whether the community will at last consciously accept the teaching of Socialism, setting itself definitely to put an end to large-scale private capitalism, and undertaking itself the direct control of industry. The intellectual outlook is bright; the principles of Socialism are already accepted by a sensible proportion of the men and women in all classes who take the trouble to think, and if we must admit that but little has yet been done, we may well believe that in the fullness of time our ideas will prevail. The present war is giving the old world a great shake, and an era of precipitated reconstruction may ensue if the opportunity be wisely handled.

The influence of the Fabian Society on political thought is already the theme of doctoral theses by graduates, especially in American universities, but it has not yet found much place in weightier compilation. Indeed so far as I know the only serious attempts in this country to describe its character and estimate its proportions is to be found in an admirable little book by Mr. Ernest Barker of New College, Oxford, entitled "Political Thought in England from Herbert Spencer to the Present Day." The author, dealing with the early Fabians, points out that "Mill rather than Marx was their starting point," but he infers from this that "they start along the line suggested by Mill with an attack on rent as the 'unearned increment' of land," a curious inaccuracy since our earliest contribution to the theory of Socialism, Tract No. 7, "Capital and Land," was expressly directed to emphasising the comparative unimportance of Land Nationalisation, and nothing in the later work of the Society has been inconsistent with this attitude. Then Mr. Barker goes on: "Fabianism began after 1884 to supply a new philosophy in place of Benthamite Individualism. Of the new gospel of collectivism a German writer has said Webb was the Bentham and Shaw the Mill. Without assigning rôles we may fairly say there is some resemblance between the influence of Benthamism on legislation after 1830 and the influence of Fabianism on legislation since, at any rate, 1906. In either case we have a small circle of thinkers and investigators in quiet touch with politicians: in either case we have a 'permeation' of general opinion by the ideas of these thinkers and investigators.... It is probable that the historian of the future will emphasise Fabianism in much the same way as the historian of to-day emphasises Benthamism."

Mr. Barker next explains that "Fabianism has its own political creed, if it is a political creed consequential upon an economic doctrine. That economic doctrine advocates the socialisation of rent. But the rents which the Fabians would socialise are not only rents from land. Rent in the sense of unearned increments may be drawn, and is drawn, from other sources. The successful entrepreneur for instance draws a rent of ability from his superior equipment and education. The socialisation of every kind of rent will necessarily arm the State with great funds which it must use.... Shaw can define the two interconnected aims of Fabianism as 'the gradual extension of the franchise and the transfer of rent and interest to the State.'"

As Mr. Barker may not be alone in a slight misinterpretation of Fabian doctrine it may be well to take this opportunity of refuting the error. He says that Fabianism advocates the socialisation of rent, and in confirmation quotes Shaw's words "rent *and interest*"! That makes all the difference. If the term rent is widened to include all differential unearned incomes, from land, from ability, from opportunity (i.e. special profits), interest includes all non-differential unearned incomes, and thus the State is to be endowed, not with rents alone, but with all unearned incomes. It is true that the Fabians, throwing over Marx's inaccurate term "surplus value," base their Socialism on the Law of Rent, because, as they allege, this law negatives both equality of income and earnings in proportion to labour, so long as private ownership of land prevails. It is also true that they have directed special attention to the unearned incomes of the "idle" landlord and shareholder, because these are the typical feature of the modern system of distribution, which indeed has come to the front since the time of Marx, and because they furnish the answer to those who contend that wealth is at present distributed approximately in accordance with personal capacity or merit, and tacitly assume that "the rich" are all of them great captains of industry who by enterprise and ability have actually created their vast fortunes. Indeed we might say that we do not mind conceding to our opponents all the wealth "created" by superior brains, if they will let us deal with the unearned incomes which are received independent of the possession of any brains, or any services at all!

But although we regard the case of the capitalist employer as relatively negligible, and although we prefer to concentrate our attack on the least defensible side of the capitalist system — and already the State recognises that unearned incomes should pay a larger proportion in income-tax, that property which passes at death, necessarily to those who have not earned it, should contribute a large quota to the public purse, and that unearned increment on land should in part belong to the public — that does not mean that we have any tenderness for the entrepreneur. Him we propose to deal with by the favourite Fabian method of municipalisation and nationalisation. We take over his "enterprise," his gasworks and waterworks, his docks and trams, his railways and mines. We secure for the State the profits of management and the future unearned increment, and we compensate him for his capital with interest-bearing securities. We force him in fact to become the idle recipient of unearned income, and then we turn round and upbraid him and tax him heavily precisely because his income is unearned! If there is any special tenderness in this treatment, I should prefer harshness. To me it seems to resemble the policy of the wolf towards the lamb.

I will proceed with quotations from Mr. Barker, because the view of a historian of thought is weightier than anything I could say.

"But collectivism also demands in the second place expert government. It demands the 'aristocracy of talent' of which Carlyle wrote. The control of a State with powers so vast will obviously need an exceptional and exceptionally large aristocracy. Those opponents of Fabianism who desire something more revolutionary than its political 'meliorism' and 'palliatives' accuse it of alliance with bureaucracy. They urge that it relies on bureaucracy to administer social reforms from above; and they conclude that, since any governing *class* is anti-democratic, the Fabians who believe in such a class are really anti-democratic. The charge seems, as a matter of fact, difficult to sustain. Fabians from the first felt and urged that the decentralisation of the State was a necessary condition of the realisation of their aim. The municipality and other local units were the natural bodies for administering the new funds and discharging the new duties which the realisation of that aim would create. 'A democratic State,' Shaw wrote, 'cannot become a Social Democratic State unless it has in every centre of population a local governing body as thoroughly democratic in its constitution as the central Parliament.' The House of Commons he felt must develop 'into the central government which will be the organ of federating the municipalities.'

Fabianism thus implied no central bureaucracy; what it demanded was partly, indeed, a more efficient and expert central government (and there is plenty of room for that), but primarily an expert local civil service in close touch with and under the control of a really democratic municipal government. It is difficult to say that this is bureaucracy or that it is not desirable. Many men who are not Fabians or Socialists of any kind feel strongly that the breathing of more vigour and interest into local politics, and the creation of a proper local civil service, are the great problems of the future.

"The policy of Fabianism has thus been somewhat as follows. An intellectual circle has sought to permeate all classes, from the top to the bottom, with a common opinion in favour of social control of socially created values. Resolved to permeate all classes, it has not preached class-consciousness; it has worked as much with and through Liberal 'capitalists' as with and through Labour representatives. Resolved gradually to permeate, it has not been revolutionary: it has relied on the slow growth of opinion. Reformist rather than revolutionary, it has explained the impossibility of the sudden 'revolution' of the working classes against capital: it has urged the necessity of a gradual amelioration of social conditions by a gradual assertion of social control over unearned increment.

"Hence Fabianism has not adopted the somewhat cold attitude of the pure Socialist Party to Trade Unions, but has rather found in their gradual conquest of better wages and better conditions for the workers the line of social advance congenial with its own principles. Again, it has preached that the society which is to exert control must be democratic, if the control is to be, as it must be, self-control: it has taught that such democratic self-control must primarily be exerted in democratic local self-government: it has emphasised the need of reconciling democratic control with expert guidance. While it has never advocated 'direct action' or the avoidance of political activity, while on the contrary, it has advocated the conquest of social reforms on the fields of parliamentary and municipal government, it has not defended the State as it is, but has rather urged the need for a State which is based on democracy tempered by respect for the 'expert.' In this way Socialism of the Fabian type has made representative democracy its creed. It has adopted the sound position that democracy flourishes in that form of state in which people freely produce, thanks to an equality of educational opportunity, and freely choose, thanks to a wide and active suffrage, their own members for their guidance, and, since they have freely produced and chosen them, give them freely and fully the honour of their trust. And thus Socialists like Mr. Sidney Webb and Mr. Ramsay Macdonald have not coquetted with primary democracy, which has always had a magnetic attraction for Socialists. The doctrine that the people itself governs directly through obedient agents—the doctrine of mandate and plebiscite, of referendum and initiative—is not the doctrine of the best English Socialism."

Mr. Barker next explains that behind these ideas lies "an organic theory of society," that society is regarded as "an organic unity with a real 'general will' of its own," and after stating that "the development of Liberalism, during the last few years, shows considerable traces of Fabian influence," concludes the subject with the words "Collectivism of the Fabian order was the dominant form of Socialism in England till within the last three of four years." Of the movement of Guild Socialists and others which he deems to have replaced it I shall speak later.

I have ventured to quote from Mr. Barker at some length because his summary of Fabian doctrine seems to me (with the exception noted) to be both correct and excellent, and it is safer to borrow from a writer quite unconnected with the Society an estimate of its place in the history of English political thought, rather than to offer my own necessarily prejudiced opinion of its achievements.

But I must revert again to the Fabian "method." "Make Socialists," said Mr. Wells in "Faults of the Fabian," "and you will achieve Socialism. There is no other way"; and Mr. Wells in his enthusiasm anticipated a society of ten thousand Fabians as the result of a year's propaganda. Will Socialism come through the making of Socialists?

If so, Socialism has made but little progress in England, since the number who profess and call themselves Socialist is still insignificant.

The foregoing pages have shown in the words of a student of political thought how Socialism has been made in England in quite another way.

We did not at the time repudiate Mr. Wells' dictum: indeed we adopted his policy, and attempted the making of Socialism on a large scale. No doubt there is a certain ambiguity in the word "Socialists." It may mean members of Socialist societies, or at any rate "unattached Socialists," all those in fact who use the name to describe their political opinions. Or it may merely be another way of stating that the existing form of society can only be altered by the wills of living people, and change will only be in the direction of Socialism, when the wills which are effective for the purpose choose that direction in preference to another.

Mr. Wells himself described as a "fantastic idea" the notion that "the world may be manoeuvred into Socialism without knowing it": that "society is to keep like it is ... and yet Socialism will be soaking through it all, changing without a sign," and he at any rate meant by his phrase, "make members of Socialist societies."

The older and better Fabian doctrine is set out in the opening paragraphs of Tract 70, the "Report on Fabian Policy" (1896).

"The Mission Of The Fabians

The object of the Fabian Society is to persuade the English people to make their political constitution thoroughly democratic and so to socialise their industries as to make the livelihood of the people entirely independent of private capitalism.

The Fabian Society endeavours to pursue its Socialist and Democratic objects with complete singleness of aim. For example:

It has no distinctive opinions on the Marriage Question, Religion, Art, abstract Economics, historic Evolution, Currency, or any other subject than its own special business of practical Democracy and Socialism.

It brings all the pressure and persuasion in its power to bear on existing forces, caring nothing by what name any party calls itself or what principles, Socialist or other, it professes, but having regard solely to the tendency of its actions, supporting those which make for Socialism and Democracy and opposing those which are reactionary.

It does not propose that the practical steps towards Social Democracy should be carried out by itself or by any other specially organised society or party.

It does not ask the English people to join the Fabian Society."

In old days acting on this view of our "mission" we deliberately allowed the Society to remain small. Latterly we tried to expand, and in the main our attempt was an expensive failure. The other Socialist bodies have always used their propaganda primarily for recruiting; and they have sought to enlist the rank and file of the British people. In this they too have substantially failed, and the forty or fifty thousand members of the I.L.P. and B.S.P. are roughly no larger a proportion of the working class than the three thousand Fabians are of the middle class. If the advance of Socialism in England is to be measured by the "making of Socialists," if we are to count membership, to enumerate meetings, to sum up subscriptions, the outlook is gloomy. Thirty-four years ago a group of strong men led by Mr. H.M. Hyndman founded the Democratic Federation, which survives as the British Socialist Party, with Mr. Hyndman still to the fore; the rest have more or less dropped out, and no one has arisen to take their places. Twenty-two years ago Keir Hardie founded the Independent Labour Party: he has died since the first draft of this passage was written, and no one is left who commands such universal affection and respect amongst the members of the Society he created. Of the seven Essayists who virtually founded the Fabian Society only one is still fully in harness, and his working life must necessarily be nearing its term. It may be doubted whether a society for the propagation of ideas has the power to long outlive the inspiration of its founder, unless indeed he is a man of such outstanding personality that his followers treat him as a god. The religions of the world have been maintained by worshippers, and even in our own day the followers of Marx have held together partly because they regard his teachings with the uncritical reverence usually accorded to the prophets of new faiths. But Marxism has survived in Germany chiefly because it has created and inspired a political party, and political parties are of a different order from propagandist societies. Socialism in England has not yet created a political party; for the Labour Party, though entirely Socialist in policy, is not so in name or in creed, and in this matter the form counts rather than the fact.

Europe, as I write in the early days of 1916, is in the melting-pot, and it would be foolish to prophesy either the fate of the nations now at war or, in particular, the future of political parties in Great Britain, and especially of the Labour Party.

But so far as concerns the Fabian Society and the two other Socialist Societies, this much may be said: three factors in the past have kept them apart: differences of temperament; differences of policy; differences of leadership. In fact perhaps the last was the strongest.

I do not mean that the founders of the three societies entertained mutual antipathies or personal jealousies to the detriment of the movement. I do mean that each group preferred to go its own way, and saw no sufficient advantage in a common path to compensate for the difficulties of selecting it.

In a former chapter I have explained how a movement for a form of Socialist Unity had at last almost achieved success, when a new factor, the European War, interposed. After the war these negotiations will doubtless be resumed, and the three Socialist Societies will find themselves more closely allied than ever before. The differences of policy which have divided them will then be a matter of past history. The differences of temperament matter less and less as the general policy becomes fixed, and in a few years the old leaders from whose disputes the general policy emerged must all have left the stage. The younger men inherit an established platform and know nothing of the old-time quarrels and distrusts. They will come together more easily. If the organised propaganda of Socialism continues — and that perhaps is not a matter of certainty — it seems to me improbable that it will be carried on for long by three separate societies. In some way or other, in England as in so many other countries, a United Socialist organisation will be constituted.

But what of the future of Fabian ideas? In a passage already quoted Mr. Barker indicates that the dominance of "Collectivism of the Fabian order" ceased three or four years ago, and he goes on to indicate that it has been replaced by an anti-state propaganda, taking various forms, Syndicalism, Guild Socialism, and the Distributivism of Mr. Belloc. It is true that Fabianism of the old type is not the last event in the history of political thought, but it is still, I venture to think, the dominant principle in political progress. Guild Socialism, whatever its worth, is a later stage. If our railways are to be managed by the Railwaymen's Union, they must first be acquired for the community by Collectivism.

This is not the place to discuss the possibilities of Guild Socialism. After all it is but a form of Socialism, and a first principle of Fabianism has always been free thought. The leading Guild Socialists resigned from the Society: they were not expelled: they attempted to coerce the rest, but no attempt was made to coerce them. Guild Socialism as a scheme for placing production under the management of the producers seems to me to be on the wrong lines. The consumer as a citizen must necessarily decide what is to be produced for his needs. But I do not belong to the generation which will have to settle the matter. The elderly are incompetent judges of new ideas. Fabian doctrine is not stereotyped: the Society consists in the main of young people. The Essayists and their contemporaries have said their say: it remains for the younger people to accept what they choose, and to add whatever is necessary. Those who repudiated the infallibility of Marx will be the last to claim infallibility for themselves. I can only express the hope that as long as the Fabian Society lasts it will be ever open to new ideas, ever conscious that nothing is final, ever aware that the world is enormously complex, and that no single formula will summarise or circumscribe its infinite variety.

The work of the Fabian Society has been not to make Socialists, but to make Socialism. I think it may be said that the dominant opinion in the Society — at any rate it is my opinion — is that great social changes can only come by consent. The Capitalist system cannot be overthrown by a revolution or by a parliamentary majority. Wage slavery will disappear, as serfdom disappeared, not indeed imperceptibly, for the world is now self-conscious, not even so gradually, for the pace of progress is faster than it was in the Middle Ages, but by a change of heart of the community, by a general recognition, already half realised, that whatever makes for the more equitable distribution of wealth is good; that whatever benefits the working class benefits the nation; that the rich exist only on sufferance, and deserve no more than painless extinction; that the capitalist is a servant of the public, and too often over-paid for the services that he renders.

Again, Socialism succeeds because it is common sense. The anarchy of individual production is already an anachronism. The control of the community over itself extends every day. We demand order, method, regularity, design; the accidents of sickness and misfortune, of old age and bereavement, must be prevented if possible, and if not, mitigated. Of this principle the public is already convinced: it is merely a question of working out the details. But order and forethought is wanted for industry as well as for human life. Competition is bad, and in most respects private monopoly is worse. No one now seriously defends the system of rival traders with their crowds of commercial travellers: of rival tradesmen with their innumerable deliveries in each street; and yet no one advocates the capitalist alternative, the great trust, often concealed and insidious, which monopolises oil or tobacco or diamonds, and makes huge profits for a fortunate few out of the helplessness of the unorganised consumers.

But neither the idle rich class nor the anarchy of competition is so outstanding an evil as the poverty of the poor. We aim at making the rich poorer chiefly in order to make the poor richer. Our first tract, "Why are the Many Poor?" struck the keynote. In a century of abounding wealth England still has in its midst a hideous mass of poverty which is too appalling to think of. That poverty, we say, is preventible. That poverty was the background of our thoughts when the Society was founded. Perhaps we have done a little to mitigate it: we believe we have done something to make clear the way by which it may ultimately be abolished. We do not constantly talk of it. We write of the advantages of Municipal Electricity, of the powers of Parish Councils, of the objections to the Referendum; but all the while it is that great evil which chiefly moves us, and by our success or our failure in helping on the reconstruction of society for the purpose of abolishing poverty, the work of the Fabian Society must ultimately be judged.

Appendix I   Memoranda by Bernard Shaw

Bernard Shaw has been good enough to write the following memoranda on Chapter XII. For various reasons I prefer to leave that chapter as it stands; but the memoranda have an interest of their own and I therefore print them here.

A   On The History Of Fabian Economics

Mr. Barker's guesses greatly underrate the number of tributaries which enlarged the trickle of Socialist thought into a mighty river. They also shew how quickly waves of thought are forgotten. Far from being the economic apostle of Socialism, Mill, in the days when the Fabian Society took the field, was regarded as the standard authority for solving the social problem by a combination of peasant proprietorship with neo-Malthusianism. The Dialectical Society, which was a centre of the most advanced thought in London until the Fabian Society supplanted it, was founded to advocate the principles of Mill's Essay on Liberty, which was much more the Bible of English Individualism than Das Kapital ever was of English Socialism. As late as 1888 Henry Sidgwick, a follower of Mill, rose indignantly at the meeting of the British Association in Bath, to which I had just read the paper on The Transition to Social-Democracy, which was subsequently published as one of the Fabian Essays, and declared that I had advocated nationalisation of land; that nationalisation of land was a crime; and that he would not take part in a discussion of a criminal proposal. With that he left the platform, all the more impressively as his apparently mild and judicial temperament made the incident so unexpected that his friends who had not actually witnessed it were with difficulty persuaded that it had really happened. It illustrates the entire failure of Mill up to that date to undo the individualistic teaching of the earlier volumes of his Political Economy by the Socialist conclusions to which his work on the treatise led him at the end. Sidney Webb astonished and confounded our Individualist opponents by citing Mill against them; and it is probably due to Webb more than to any other disciple that it is now generally known that Mill died a Socialist. Webb read Mill and mastered Mill as he seemed to have read and mastered everybody else; but the only other prominent Socialist who can be claimed by Mill as a convert was, rather unexpectedly, William Morris, who said that when he read the passage in which Mill, after admitting that the worst evils of Communism are, compared to the evils of our Commercialism, as dust in the balance, nevertheless condemned Communism, he immediately became a Communist, as Mill had clearly given his verdict against the evidence. Except in these instances we heard nothing of Mill in the Fabian Society. Cairnes's denunciation of the idle consumers of rent and interest was frequently quoted; and Marshall's Economics of Industry was put into our book boxes as a textbook; but the taste for abstract economics was no more general in the Fabian Society than elsewhere. I had in my boyhood read some of Mill's detached essays, including those on constitutional government and on the Irish land question, as well as the inevitable one on Liberty; but none of these pointed to Socialism; and my attention was first drawn to political economy as the science of social salvation by Henry George's eloquence, and by his Progress and Poverty, which had an enormous circulation in the early eighties, and beyond all question had more to do with the Socialist revival of that period in England than any other book. Before the Fabian Society existed I pressed George's propaganda of Land Nationalisation on a meeting of the Democratic Federation, but was told to read Karl Marx. I was so complete a novice in economics at that time that when I wrote a letter to Justice pointing out a flaw in Marx's reasoning, I regarded my letter merely as a joke, and fully expected that some more expert Socialist economist would refute me easily. Even when the refutation did not arrive I remained so impressed with the literary power and overwhelming documentation of Marx's indictment of nineteenth-century Commercialism and the capitalist system, that I defended him against all comers in and out of season until Philip Wicksteed, the well-known Dante commentator, then a popular Unitarian minister, brought me to a standstill by a criticism of Marx which I did not understand. This was the first appearance in Socialist controversy of the value theory of Jevons, published in 1871. Professor Edgeworth and Mr. Wicksteed, to whom Jevons appealed as a mathematician, were at that time trying to convince the academic world of the importance of Jevons's theory; but I, not being a mathematician, was not easily accessible to their methods of demonstration. I consented to reply to Mr. Wicksteed on the express condition that the editor of To-day, in which my reply appeared, should find space for a rejoinder by Mr. Wicksteed. My reply, which was not bad for a fake, and contained the germ of the economic argument for equality of income which I put forward twenty-five years later, elicited only a brief rejoinder; but the upshot was that I put myself into Mr. Wicksteed's hands and became a convinced Jevonian, fascinated by the subtlety of Jevons's theory and the exquisiteness with which it adapted itself to all the cases which had driven previous economists, including Marx, to take refuge in clumsy distinctions between use value, exchange value, labour value, supply and demand value, and the rest of the muddlements of that time.

Accordingly, the abstract economics of the Fabian Essays are, as regards value, the economics of Jevons. As regards rent they are the economics of Ricardo, which I, having thrown myself into the study of abstract economics, had learnt from Ricardo's own works and from De Quincey's Logic of Political Economy. I maintained, as I still do, that the older economists, writing before Socialism had arisen as a possible alternative to Commercialism and a menace to its vested interests, were far more candid in their statements and thorough in their reasoning than their successors, and was fond of citing the references in De Quincey and Austin's Lectures on Jurisprudence to the country gentleman system and the evils of capitalism, as instances of frankness upon which no modern professor dare venture.

The economical and moral identity of capital and interest with land and rent was popularly demonstrated by Olivier in Tract 7 on Capital and Land, and put into strict academic form by Sidney Webb. The point was of importance at a time when the distinction was still so strongly maintained that the Fabian Society was compelled to exclude Land Nationalizers, both before and after their development into Single Taxers, because they held that though land and rent should be socialized, capital and interest must remain private property.

This really exhausts the history of the Fabian Society as far as abstract economic theory is concerned. Activity in that department was confined to Webb and myself. Later on, Pease's interest in banking and currency led him to contribute some criticism of the schemes of the currency cranks who infest all advanced movements, flourishing the paper money of the Guernsey Market, and to give the Society some positive guidance as to the rapid integration of modern banking. But this was an essay in applied economics. It may be impossible to draw a line between the old abstract deductive economics and the modern historical concrete economics; but the fact remains that though the water may be the same, the tide has turned. A comparison of my exposition of the law of rent in my first Fabian Essay and in my Impossibilities of Anarchism with the Webbs' great Histories of Trade Unionism and of Industrial Democracy will illustrate the difference between the two schools.

The departure was made by Graham Wallas, who, abandoning the deductive construction of intellectual theorems, made an exhaustive study of the Chartist movement. It is greatly to be regretted that these lectures were not effectively published. Their delivery wrought a tremendous disillusion as to the novelty of our ideas and methods of propaganda; much new gospel suddenly appeared to us as stale failure; and we recognized that there had been weak men before Agamemnon, even as far back as in Cromwell's army. The necessity for mastering the history of our own movement and falling into our ordered place in it became apparent; and it was in this new frame of mind that the monumental series of works by the Webbs came into existence. Wallas's Life of Francis Place shows his power of reconstructing a popular agitation with a realism which leaves the conventional imaginary version of it punctured and flaccid; and it was by doing the same for the Chartist movement that he left his mark on us.

Of the other Essayists, Olivier had wrestled with the huge Positive Philosophy of Comte, who thus comes in as a Fabian influence. William Clarke was a disciple of Mazzini, and found Emerson, Thoreau, and the Brook Farm enthusiasts congenial to him. Bland, who at last became a professed Catholic, was something of a

Coleridgian transcendentalist, though he treated a copy of Bakunin's God and the State to a handsome binding. Mrs. Besant's spiritual history has been written by herself. Wallas brought to bear a wide scholastic culture of the classic type, in which modern writers, though interesting, were not fundamental. The general effect, it will be perceived, is very much wider and more various than that suggested by Mr. Ernest Barker's remark that Mill was our starting point.

It is a curious fact that of the three great propagandist amateurs of political economy, Henry George, Marx, and Ruskin, Ruskin alone seems to have had no effect on the Fabians. Here and there in the Socialist movement workmen turned up who had read Fors Clavigera or Unto This Last; and some of the more well-to-do no doubt had read the first chapter of Munera Pulveris. But Ruskin's name was hardly mentioned in the Fabian Society. My explanation is that, barring Olivier, the Fabians were inveterate Philistines. My efforts to induce them to publish Richard Wagner's Art and Revolution, and, later on, Oscar Wilde's The Soul of Man under Socialism, or even to do justice to Morris's News From Nowhere, fell so flat that I doubt whether my colleagues were even conscious of them. Our best excuse must be that as a matter of practical experience English political societies do good work and present a dignified appearance whilst they attend seriously to their proper political business; but, to put it bluntly, they make themselves ridiculous and attract undesirables when they affect art and philosophy. The Arts and Crafts exhibitions, the Anti-Scrape (Society for the Protection of Ancient Buildings), and the Art Workers' Guild, under Morris and Crane, kept up a very intimate connection between Art and Socialism; but the maintenance of Fabian friendly relations with them was left mostly to me and Stewart Headlam. The rest kept aloof and consoled themselves with the reflection—if they thought about it at all—that the Utilitarians, though even more Philistine than the Fabians, were astonishingly effective for their numbers.

It must be added that though the tradition that Socialism excludes the established creeds was overthrown by the Fabians, and the claim of the Christian Socialists to rank with the best of us was insisted on faithfully by them, the Fabian leaders did not break the tradition in their own practice. The contention of the Anti-Socialist Union that all Socialists are atheists is no doubt ridiculous in the face of the fact that the intellectual opposition to Socialism has been led exclusively by avowed atheists like Charles Bradlaugh or agnostics like Herbert

Spencer, whilst Communism claims Jesus as an exponent; still, if the question be raised as to whether any of the Fabian Essayists attended an established place of worship regularly, the reply must be in the negative. Indeed, they were generally preaching themselves on Sundays. To describe them as irreligious in view of their work would be silly; but until Hubert Bland towards the end of his life took refuge in the Catholic Church, and Mrs. Besant devoted herself to Theosophy, no leading Fabian found a refuge for his soul in the temples of any established denomination. I may go further and admit that the first problems the Fabians had to solve were so completely on the materialist plane that the atmosphere inevitably became uncongenial to those whose capacity was wasted and whose sympathies were starved on that plane. Even psychical research, with which Pease and Podmore varied their Fabian activities, tended fatally towards the exposure of alleged psychical phenomena as physical tricks. The work that came to our hands in our first two decades was materialistic work; and it was not until the turn of the century brought us the Suffrage movement and the Wells raid, that the materialistic atmosphere gave way, and the Society began to retain recruits of a kind that it always lost in the earlier years as it lost Mrs. Besant and (virtually) William Clarke. It is certainly perceptibly less hard-headed than it was in its first period.

B   On Guild Socialism

Here I venture to say, with some confidence, that Mr. Barker is mistaken. That storm has burst on the Fabian Society and has left it just where it was. Guild Socialism, championed by the ablest and most industrious insurgents of the rising generation in the Society, raised its issue with Collectivism only to discover, when the matter, after a long agitation, was finally thrashed out at a conference at Barrow House, that the issue was an imaginary one, and that Collectivism lost nothing by the fullest tenable concessions to the Guild Socialists. A very brief consideration will shew that this was inevitable.

Guild Socialism, in spite of its engaging medieval name, means nothing more picturesque than a claim that under Socialism each industry shall be controlled by its own operators, as the professions are to-day. This by itself would not imply Socialism at all: it would be merely a revival of the medieval guild, or a fresh attempt at the now exploded self-governing workshop of the primitive co-operators. Guild Socialism, with the emphasis on the Socialism, implies that the industries, however completely they may be controlled by their separate staffs, must pool their products. All the Guild Socialists admit this. The Socialist State must therefore include an organ for receiving and distributing the pooled products; and such an organ, representing the citizen not as producer but as consumer, reintroduces the whole machinery of Collectivism. Thus the alleged antithesis between Guild Socialism and Collectivism, under cover of which the one was presented as an alternative to the other, vanished at the first touch of the skilled criticism the Fabians brought to bear on it; and now Mrs. Sidney Webb, who was singled out for attack by the Guild Socialists as the arch Collectivist, is herself conducting an investigation into the existing control of industry by professional organizations, whilst the quondam Guild Socialists are struggling with the difficult question of the proper spheres of the old form of Trade Union now called the craft union, and the new form called the industrial union, in which workers of all crafts and occupations, from clerks and railway porters to locomotive drivers and fitters, are organized in a single union of the entire industry. There is work enough for many years to some of the old Fabian kind in these directions; and this work will irresistibly reunite the disputants instead of perpetuating a quarrel in which, like most of the quarrels which the Society has survived, there was nothing fundamental at issue.

There is work, too, to be done in the old abstract deductive department. It can be seen, throughout the history of the Society, how any attempt to discard the old economic basis of the law of rent immediately produced a recrudescence of Anarchism in one form or another, the latest being Syndicalism and that form of Guild Socialism which was all Guild and no Socialism. But there is still much to be settled by the deductive method. The fundamental question of the proportions in which the national income, when socialized, shall be distributed, was not grappled with until 1914, when I, lecturing on behalf of the Society, delivered my final conclusion that equal distribution is the only solution that will realize the ideals of Socialism, and that it is in fact the economic goal of Socialism. This is not fully accepted as yet in the movement, in which there is still a strong leaven of the old craving for an easy-going system which, beginning with "the socialization of the means of production, distribution, and exchange," will then work out automatically without interference with the citizen's private affairs.

Another subject which has hardly yet been touched, and which also must begin with deductive treatment, is what may be called the democratization of democracy, and its extension from a mere negative and very uncertain check on tyranny to a positive organizing force. No experienced Fabian believes that society can be reconstructed (or rather constructed; for the difficulty is that society is as yet only half rescued from chaos) by men of the type produced by popular election under existing circumstances, or indeed under any circumstances likely to be achieved before the reconstruction. The fact that a hawker cannot ply his trade without a licence whilst a man may sit in Parliament without any relevant qualifications is a typical and significant anomaly which will certainly not be removed by allowing everybody to be a hawker at will. Sooner or later, unless democracy is to be discarded in a reaction of disgust such as killed it in ancient Athens, democracy itself will demand that only such men should be presented to its choice as have proved themselves qualified for more serious and disinterested work than "stoking up" election meetings to momentary and foolish excitement. Without qualified rulers a Socialist State is impossible; and it must not be forgotten (though the reminder is as old as Plato) that the qualified men may be very reluctant men instead of very ambitious ones.

Here, then, are two very large jobs already in sight to occupy future Fabians. Whether they will call themselves Fabians and begin by joining the Fabian Society is a question which will not be settled by the generation to which I belong.

G.B.S.

Appendix II The Basis of the Fabian Society

The Fabian Society consists of Socialists.

It therefore aims at the reorganisation of Society by the emancipation of Land and Industrial Capital from individual and class ownership, and the vesting of them in the community for the general benefit. In this way only can the natural and acquired advantages of the country be equitably shared by the whole people.

The Society accordingly works for the extinction of private property in Land and of the consequent individual appropriation, in the form of Rent, of the price paid for permission to use the earth, as well as for the advantages of superior soils and sites.

The Society, further, works for the transfer to the community of the administration of such industrial Capital as can conveniently be managed socially. For, owing to the monopoly of the means of production in the past, industrial inventions and the transformation of surplus income into Capital have mainly enriched the proprietary class, the worker being now dependent on that class for leave to earn a living.

If these measures be carried out, without compensation (though not without such relief to expropriated individuals as may seem fit to the community), Rent and Interest will be added to the reward of labour, the idle class now living on the labour of others will necessarily disappear, and practical equality of opportunity will be maintained by the spontaneous action of economic forces with much less interference with personal liberty than the present system entails.

For the attainment of these ends the Fabian Society looks to the spread of Socialist opinions, and the social and political changes consequent thereon, *including the establishment of equal citizenship for men and women.* It seeks to achieve these ends by the general dissemination of knowledge as to the relation between the individual and Society in its economic, ethical, and political aspects.

LaVergne, TN USA
12 October 2010
200485LV00007B/129/P